Park and
venture,
explore, discover

$33.27
ocn173748279
[Library ed.]   08/20/2009

DENALI
NATIONAL PARK AND PRESERVE

ADVENTURE, EXPLORE, DISCOVER

DAVID ARETHA

MyReportLinks.com Books
an imprint of

Enslow Publishers, Inc. E
Box 398, 40 Industrial Road
Berkeley Heights, NJ 07922
USA

MyReportLinks.com Books, an imprint of Enslow Publishers, Inc. MyReportLinks®
is a registered trademark of Enslow Publishers, Inc.

Library of Congress Cataloging-in-Publication Data

Aretha, David.
  Denali National Park and Preserve : adventure, explore, discover / David Aretha.
      p. cm. — (America's national parks)
  Summary: "A virtual tour of Denali National Park and Preserve, with chapters devoted to the
history of this Alaska region, history of the park, plant and animal life, environmental problems
facing the park, and activities in the area"—Provided by publisher.
  Includes bibliographical references and index.
  ISBN-13: 978-1-59845-089-7 (hardcover)
  ISBN-10: 1-59845-089-1 (hardcover)
  1. Denali National Park and Preserve (Alaska)—Juvenile literature. I. Title.
F912.M23A74 2009
979.8'3—dc22
                                    2007039046

Printed in the United States of America

10 9 8 7 6 5 4 3 2 1

To Our Readers:
Through the purchase of this book, you and your library gain access to the Report Links that specifically
back up this book.
The Publisher will provide access to the Report Links that back up this book and will keep these Report
Links up to date on **www.myreportlinks.com** for five years from the book's first publication date.
We have done our best to make sure all Internet addresses in this book were active and appropriate when
we went to press. However, the author and the Publisher have no control over, and assume no liability
for, the material available on those Internet sites or on other Web sites they may link to.
The usage of the MyReportLinks.com Books Web site is subject to the terms and conditions stated on the
Usage Policy Statement on **www.myreportlinks.com**.
A password may be required to access the Report Links that back up this book. The password is found on
the bottom of page 4 of this book.
Any comments or suggestions can be sent by e-mail to comments@myreportlinks.com or to the address
on the back cover.

♻ Enslow Publishers, Inc., is committed to printing our books on recycled paper. The paper in every
book contains 10% to 30% post-consumer waste (PCW). The cover board on the outside of each book
contains 100% PCW. Our goal is to do our part to help young people and the environment too!

Photo Credits: ABC/Kane Productions, p. 58; Access Genealogy, p. 23; Alaska Department of Fish &
Game, pp. 62, 75; Alaska Department of Natural Resources, p. 96; Alaska Humanities Forum, p. 46;
Alaska's Digital Archives, p. 39; Alaska Wildlife Alliance, p. 42; © 1998–2008 Harry Kikstra,
7summits.com, p. 15; Discovery Education, p. 25; Denali Foundation, p. 32; International Arctic Research
Center, pp. 60, 79; Karen A. Lemke, p. 21; Library of Congress, p. 22; Morris Magazine Network, p. 93;
MyReportLinks.com Books, p. 4; National Park Service, pp. 5, 9, 29, 88, 98; NPCA, p. 81; PBS
Online/WGBH, p. 83; Shutterstock. com, pp. 1, 3, 6–7, 8–9, 12–13, 18–19, 26–27, 30–31, 36, 44, 52,
64–65; 68–69, 72–73, 76, 86, 90–91, 94, 97, 100–101, 104, 108, 110, 112–113; Smithsonian Institution
Department of Paleobiology, p. 84; Smithsonian National Museum of Natural History, p. 71; Travel Alaska,
p. 117; United Nations, p. 49; University of Texas Libraries, p. 50; University of Washington Libraries, p. 40;
University of Wisconsin, Board of Regents, p. 55; U.S. Department of Transportation, Federal Highway
Administration, p. 16; WWF, p. 57.

Cover Photo: Shutterstock.com

CONTENTS

MyReportLinks.com Books
Great Books, Great Links, Great for Research!

The Internet sites featured in this book can save you hours of research time. These Internet sites—we call them **"Report Links"**—are constantly changing, but we keep them up to date on our Web site.

When you see this "Approved Web Site" logo, you will know that we are directing you to a great Internet site that will help you with your research.

Give it a try! Type http://www.myreportlinks.com into your browser, click on the series title and enter the password, then click on the book title, and scroll down to the Report Links listed for this book.

The Report Links will bring you to great source documents, photographs, and illustrations. MyReportLinks.com Books save you time, feature Report Links that are kept up to date, and make report writing easier than ever! A complete listing of the Report Links can be found on pages 118–119 at the back of the book.

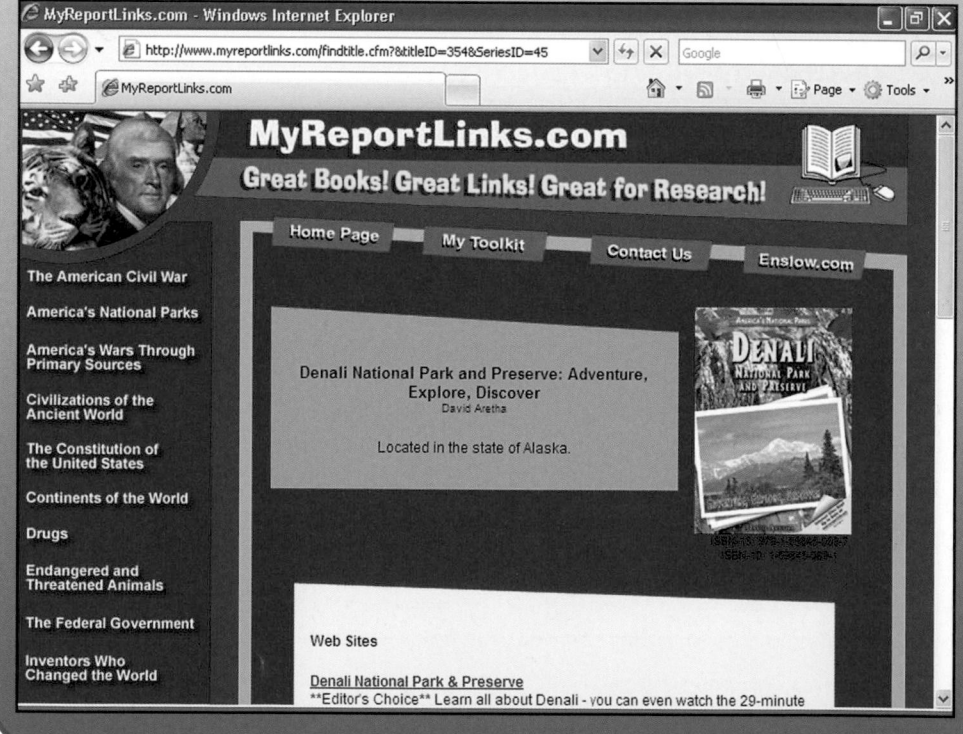

Please see "To Our Readers" on the copyright page for important information about this book, the MyReportLinks.com Web site, and the Report Links that back up this book.

Please enter **DNP1486** if asked for a password.

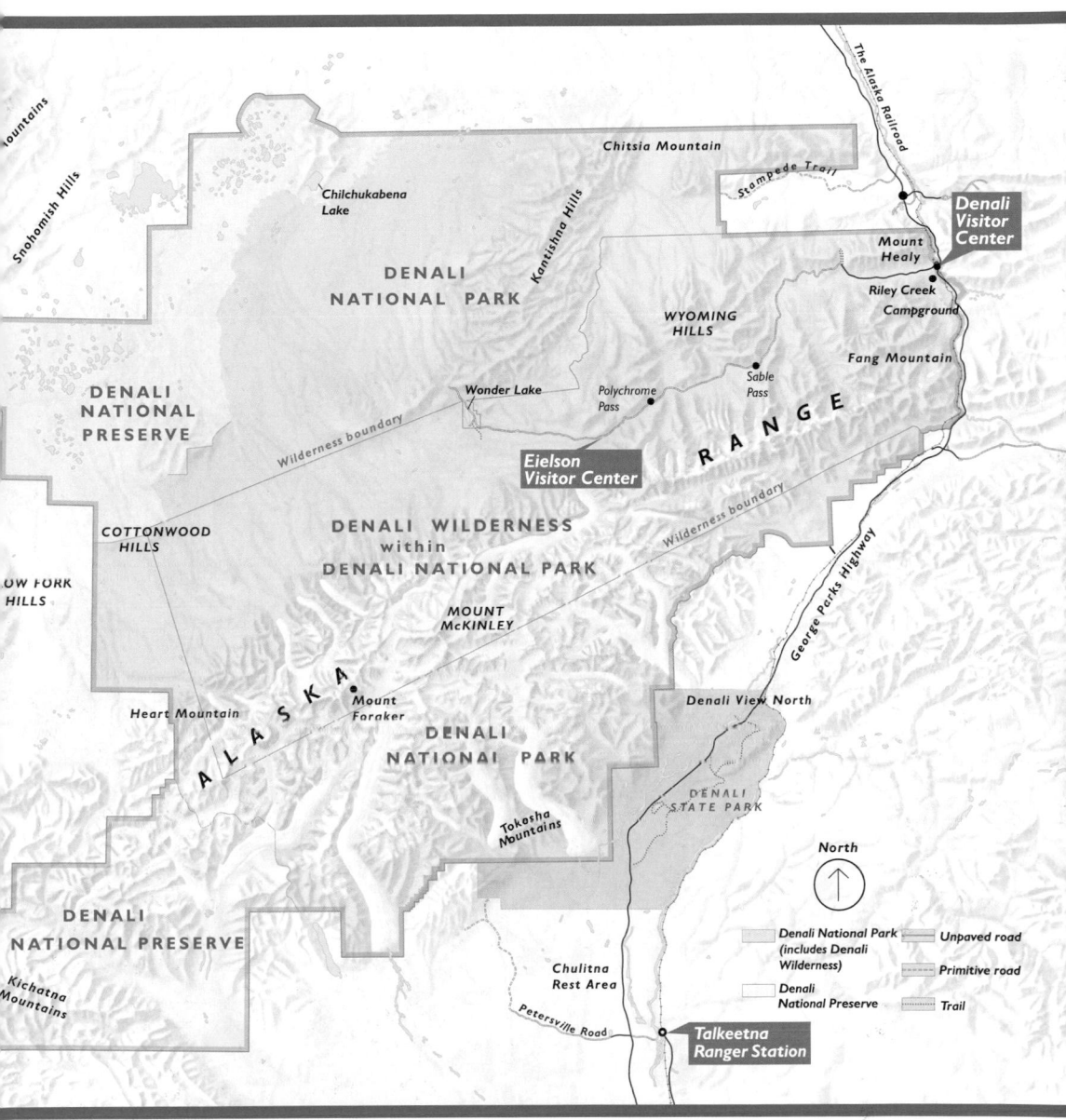

The Alaska Railroad

Chitsia Mountain

Chilchukabena
Lake

Kantishna Hills

DENALI
NATIONAL PARK

Stampede Trail

Denali
Visitor
Center

Mount
Healy

Riley Creek
Campground

Snohomish Hills

Mountains

WYOMING
HILLS

Fang Mountain

DENALI
NATIONAL
PRESERVE

Wonder Lake

Polychrome
Pass

Sable
Pass

Wilderness boundary

Eielson
Visitor Center

R   A   N   G   E

COTTONWOOD
HILLS

DENALI WILDERNESS
within
DENALI NATIONAL PARK

Wilderness boundary

George Parks Highway

OW FORK
HILLS

MOUNT
McKINLEY

Heart Mountain

A   L   A   S   K   A

Mount
Foraker

DENALI
NATIONAL PARK

Denali View North

DENALI
STATE PARK

Tokosha
Mountains

DENALI
NATIONAL PRESERVE

North

Kichatna
Mountains

Chulitna
Rest Area

Petersville Road

Talkeetna
Ranger Station

Denali National Park
(includes Denali
Wilderness)

Unpaved road

Denali
National Preserve

Primitive road

Trail

▲ This map shows Denali National Park and Preserve as well as some of
its main points of interest.

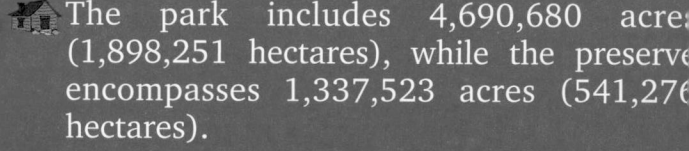

DENALI NATIONAL PARK

- Mt. McKinley National Park became the United States' thirteenth national park on February 26, 1917.

- Its name was changed to Denali National Park & Preserve on December 2, 1980. On that date, it was expanded from approximately 2 million acres (809,371 hectares) to its current 6,028,203 acres (2,439,527 hectares).

- The park includes 4,690,680 acres (1,898,251 hectares), while the preserve encompasses 1,337,523 acres (541,276 hectares).

- The perimeter of the park and preserve measures 605 miles (974 kilometers).

- Denali NP&P contains 12,130 lakes and ponds and 18,679 miles (30,061 kilometers) of streams.

- Mt. McKinley is the tallest mountain in North America (20,320 feet, 6,194 meters).

- Mt. Foraker is Denali NP&P's second tallest mountain (17,400 feet, 5,304 meters).

- The lowest elevation is at the Yentna River (200 feet, 61 meters).

- Chilchukabena Lake is Denali's largest body of water [2.6 miles long (4.2 kilometers), 2.0 miles (3.2 kilometers) wide].

- Approximately 17 percent of Denali's land is covered with glaciers.

- Denali experiences approximately six hundred small earthquakes per year.

- The highest and lowest temperatures ever recorded at Denali are 91°F and -55°F.

- Denali averages about eighty inches (203 centimeters) of snow per year.

- The park receives twenty hours, forty-nine minutes of daylight on the summer solstice (June 21) and four hours, twenty-one minutes of daylight on the winter solstice (December 21).

- Denali is home to 167 species of birds, 39 species of mammals, 10 species of fish, one species of amphibians, and zero reptiles.

- Roughly a thousand people attempt to climb Mt. McKinley each year. About half of them reach the summit.

- Close to one hundred people have died attempting to climb Mt. McKinley.

- Denali welcomes about 400,000 visitors per year.

- Denali's staff includes approximately one hundred full-time National Park Service employees and several hundred volunteers and part-time workers.

- The park road stretches 92 miles (148.1 kilometers), of which the first 14 miles (22.5 kilometers) are paved.

- Denali was designated a Biosphere Reserve Site in 1976.

- Contact information:
  Denali National Park
  P.O. Box 9
  Denali National Park, AK 99755-0009
  (907) 683-2294

Chapter 1

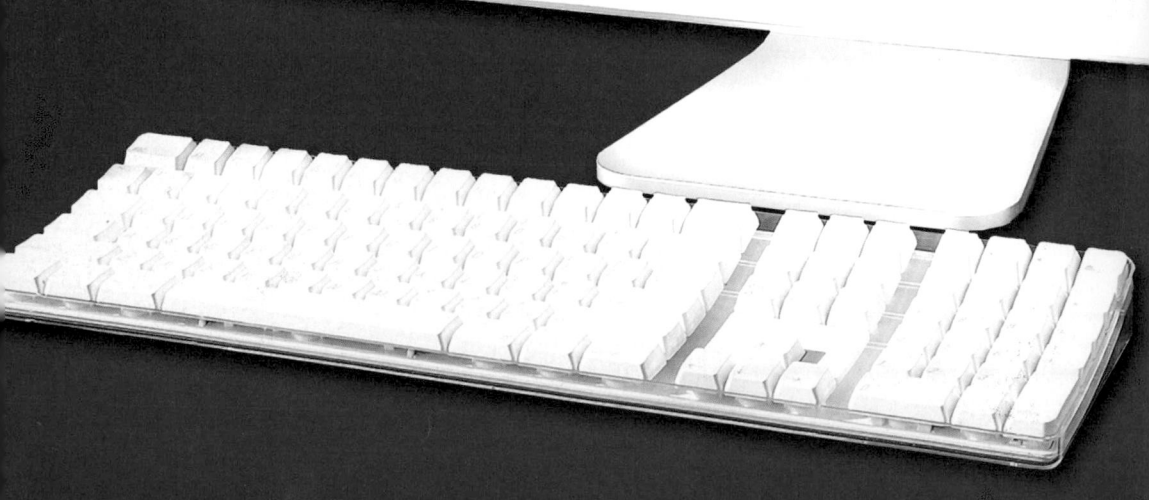

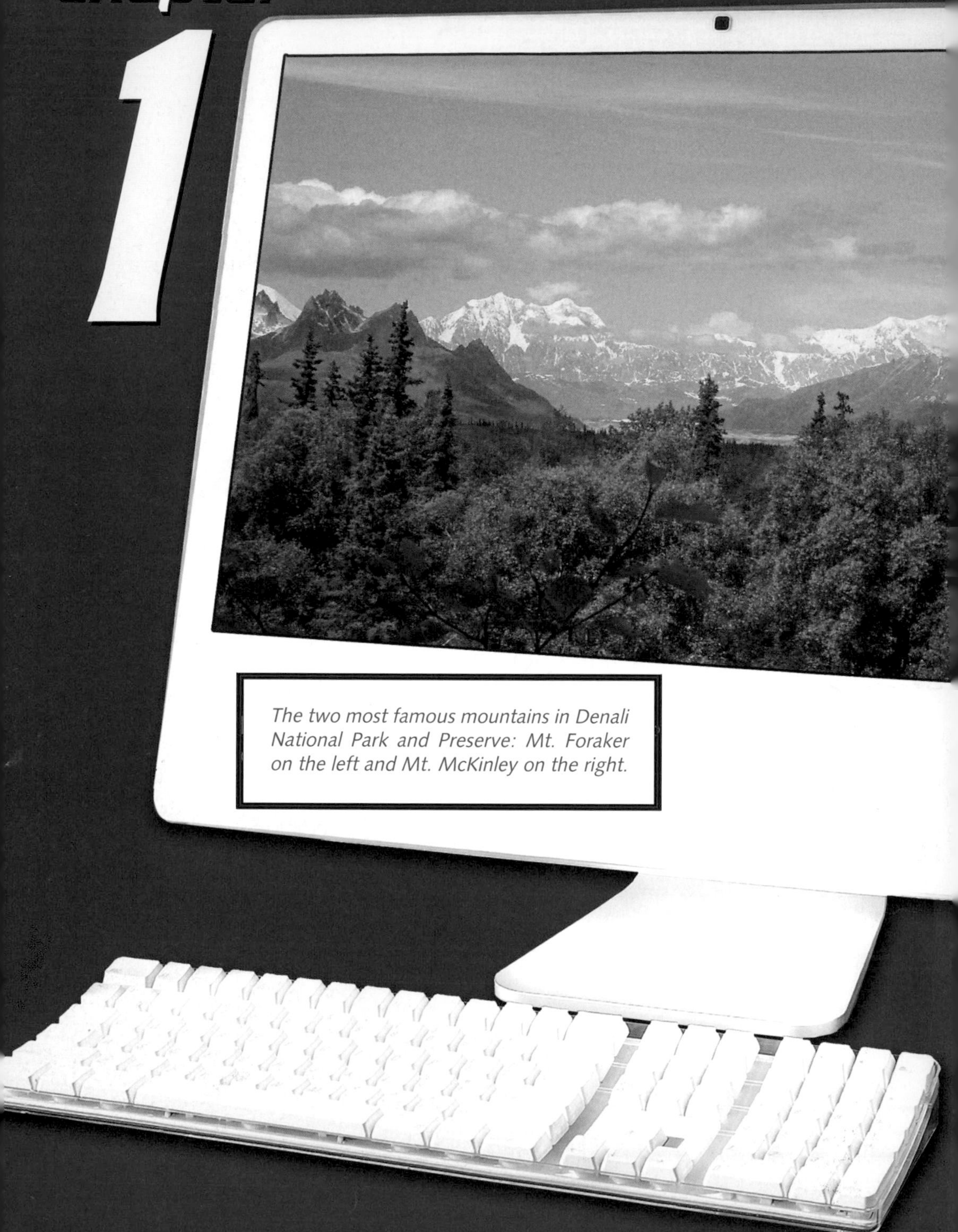

The two most famous mountains in Denali National Park and Preserve: Mt. Foraker on the left and Mt. McKinley on the right.

The High One

In 1906 a Christian missionary named Hudson Stuck became infatuated with Mt. McKinley. The Episcopal archdeacon had devoted his life to helping the American Indians of Alaska. But the sight of the magnificent wonder rekindled his old passion for mountain climbing.

"[I]t shimmered in its pearly beauty and grew clearer and brighter as I gazed," Stuck wrote. "What a glorious, broad, massive uplift that mountain is! It is not a peak, but a region. I would rather climb that mountain than discover the richest goldmine in Alaska."[1]

Stuck's dream was mighty big, for this was no ordinary mountain. Mt. McKinley, the center-piece of what eventually would become Alaska's first national park, was the tallest mountain in North America. Locals called it Denali, an Athabascan word meaning the "High One." No climber had ever reached the summit of this 20,320-foot behemoth.

Yet in 1913, a fifty-year-old Stuck embraced the challenge with three fellow climbers—Harry Karstens (age thirty-four) and a pair of twenty-one-year-olds, Robert Tatum and Walter Harper. Beginning on St. Patrick's Day, two assistants and fourteen sled-pulling dogs helped the climbers up the mountain—at least some of the way.

On April 10 the Stuck party made camp at 4,000 feet (1,219 meters). Next came a monumental challenge. For the next 8,000 feet (2,438 meters), they had to traverse Muldrow Glacier. Ascending ice and snow, the four men and six dogs lugged supplies and firewood. Afternoons in the sun could be hot, but the nights were always bitterly cold. Under their moccasins, they wore several pairs of socks. While climbing the glacier, they worried about falling into chasms, which couldn't be seen due to the covering of snow. At one point, a fire in their tent destroyed much of their food (including raisins and dried milk) as well as a sack of socks and gloves.

After somehow conquering the Muldrow Glacier, the team faced a long climb up a steep slope. Out of rock, snow, and shattered ice they carved a "staircase" that they ascended over a three-week period. They heard the rumbles of avalanches and falling ice, but the determined quartet continued skyward. The higher they climbed, the more difficult it became to breathe. Wrote Stuck: "Those

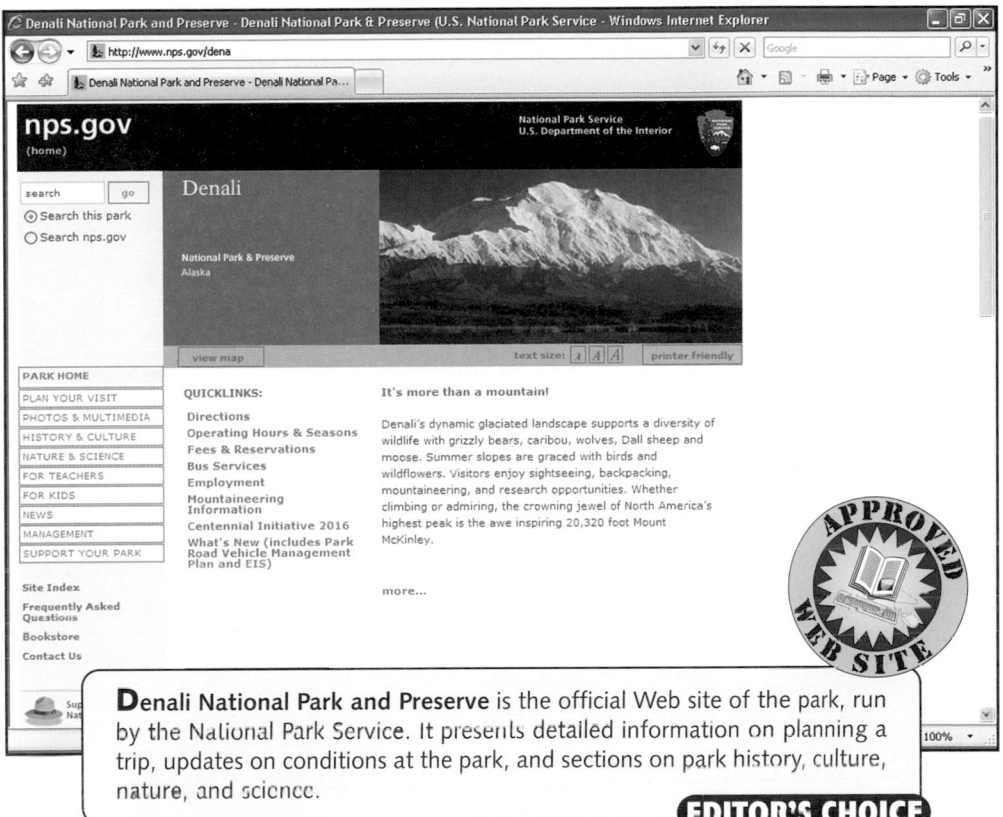

Denali National Park and Preserve is the official Web site of the park, run by the National Park Service. It presents detailed information on planning a trip, updates on conditions at the park, and sections on park history, culture, nature, and science.

EDITOR'S CHOICE

who have carried a pack only on the lower levels cannot conceive how enormously greater the labor is at these heights."[2]

On the morning of June 7, three of the men felt ill from mountain sickness, while Karstens was suffering from a severe headache. Yet that day, the party was determined to complete its ascent to the summit. Around 1:30 P.M., Harper became the first person to reach the top of the mountain. Karstens and Tatum followed, but an exhausted Stuck had to be hauled up the last few feet by rope. Stuck fell

A breathtaking vista of the Alaska Mountain Range.

unconscious for a moment, but he awoke to find that his dream had come true.

Nearly four miles (6.4 kilometers) above sea level, the four men gazed at the awesome spectacle around them. They saw Mt. Foraker, the second highest peak in Alaska. They observed the crescent shape of the Alaska Range. This long stretch of mountains would become the backbone of Denali National Park & Preserve (NP&P). That night, Stuck confided in his diary, "I remember no day in my life so full of toil, distress and exhaustion, and yet so full of happiness and keen gratification."[3]

UNTAMED WILDERNESS

In a sense, most visitors to Denali National Park & Preserve share Hudson Stuck's feelings. Denali welcomes 400,000 visitors a year, but this is rugged country and not for the faint of heart. Except for near the park entrance, hikers have no well-maintained trails on which to trek—only untamed wilderness. Temperatures plunge far below zero in the winter, and even dip into the 30s during the summer. Daylight seems endless in June and July, while darkness prevails in the dead of winter. The sparsity of trails makes it easy to get lost. Signs throughout the park warn of grizzly bears and ferocious animals—a fear that preoccupies everyone's thoughts.

Yet the rewards of the Denali experience are immeasurable: pure air and the breathtaking vista

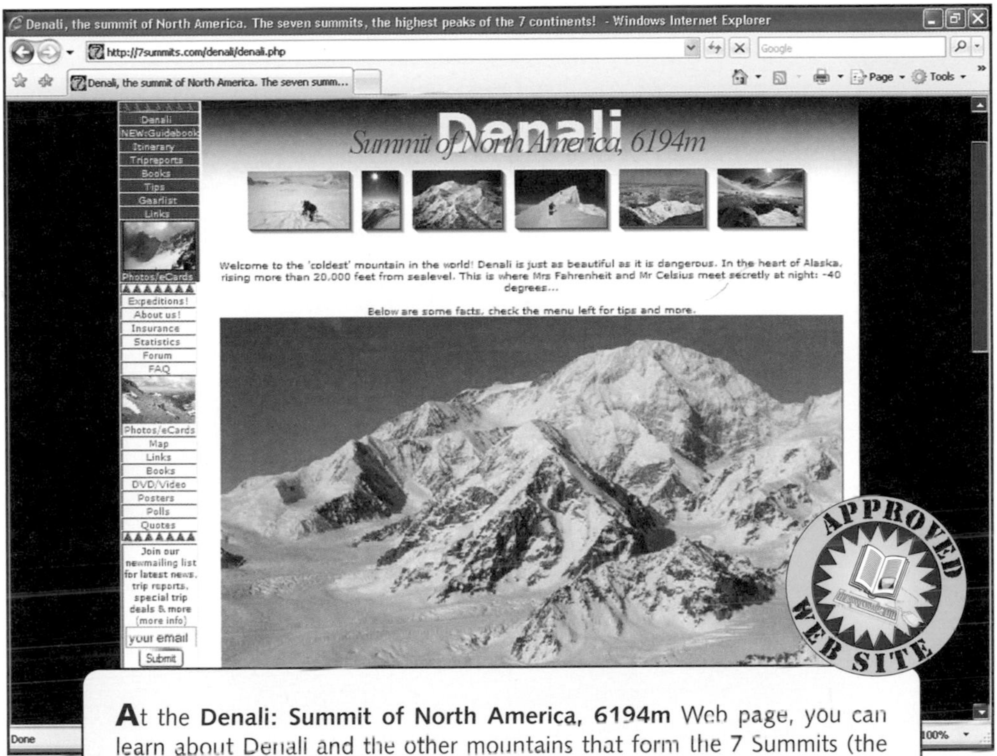

Denali, the summit of North America. The seven summits, the highest peaks of the 7 continents! - Windows Internet Explorer

http://7summits.com/denali/denali.php

Google

Denali, the summit of North America. The seven summ...

Page ▾ Tools ▾

Denali
NEW:Guidebook
Itinerary
Tripreports
Books
Tips
Gearlist
Links

Photos/eCards
▲▲▲▲▲▲▲
Expeditions!
About us!
Insurance
Statistics
Forum
FAQ

Photos/eCards
Map
Links
Books
DVD/Video
Posters
Polls
Quotes
▲▲▲▲▲▲▲
Join our
newmailing list
for latest news,
trip reports,
special trip
deals & more
(more info)

your email

Submit

Denali
Summit of North America, 6194m

Welcome to the 'coldest' mountain in the world! Denali is just as beautiful as it is dangerous. In the heart of Alaska, rising more than 20,000 feet from sealevel. This is where Mrs Fahrenheit and Mr Celsius meet secretly at night: -40 degrees...

Below are some facts, check the menu left for tips and more.

At the **Denali: Summit of North America, 6194m** Web page, you can learn about Denali and the other mountains that form the 7 Summits (the highest peaks on each continent). The site, created by expedition guides, offers pictures, expedition information, and a forum for climbers.

Done

100%

of the Alaska Range. The silhouette of an antlered moose or caribou. The piercing howl of a wolf at sunset. A golden eagle soaring above. And during the summertime, a landscape emblazoned by colorful wildflowers.

Wrote naturalist Adolph Murie, "Even without [the mountain, the park] would be outstanding because of its alpine scenery, its arctic vegetation, and its wildlife. I have walked over the green, flowering slopes in the rain, when the fog hid the

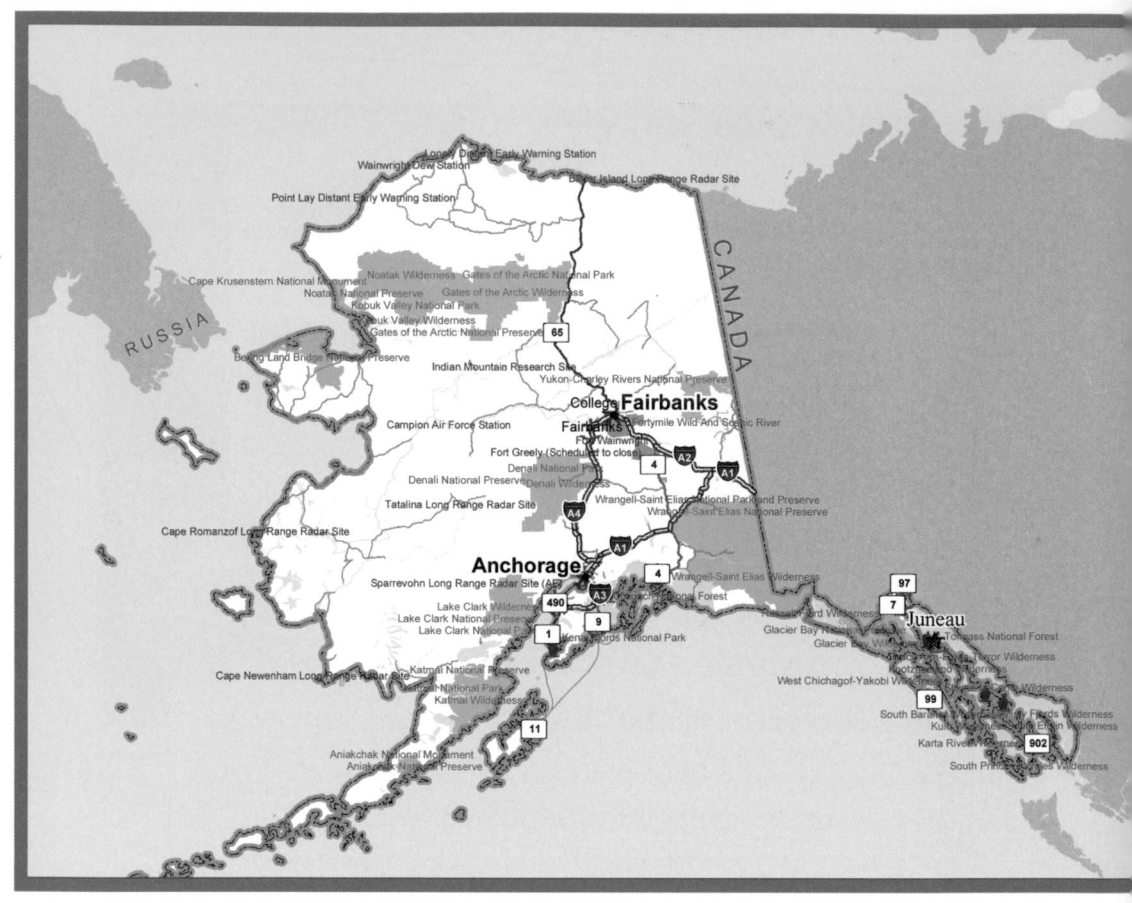

▲ Denali National Park and Preserve is located in the center of Alaska, between the cities of Anchorage and Fairbanks.

landscape beyond a few hundred yards, and felt that the white mountain avens, the purple rhodo-dendrons, and the delicate white bells of the heather at my feet were alone worthy of our efforts."[4]

⊜ BIGGER THAN NEW HAMPSHIRE

Denali National Park & Preserve comprises an enormous section of America's biggest state.

Located in south central Alaska, it covers 6,028,203 acres (2,439,527 hectares)—or 9,419 square miles (24,395 square kilometers). For comparison, New Hampshire is comprised of only 9,279 square miles (24,302 square kilometers), and Massachusetts 8,284 (21,455 square kilometers). Only a single road meanders through Denali, and less than fifteen of its ninety-two miles (148 kilometers) are paved. Mostly, it is untamed, subarctic wilderness dominated by mountains, glaciers, and water. Denali features thousands of lakes and ponds, and the length of its streams can wrap most of the way around the world.

The region was established as a national park in 1917, but its human history dates back at least twelve thousand years. To learn how the Alaska Range and Mt. McKinley evolved, we must go back much further. The story begins millions and millions of years ago.

Chapter 2

Glaciers sculpted the land that is now Denali National Park and Preserve. This is an image of a remaining glacier in the park.

Discovering Denali

Long before it was dubbed Mount McKinley, the Athabascan called the great mountain Denali. According to this Alaskan tribe, the mountain evolved as the result of a battle between two magical warriors. As legend has it, the war chief Totson (a raven) pursued his enemy, Yako, down a river. When Totson flung a spear at him, Yako turned a giant wave into stone to protect himself. This stone wave became the Denali mountain.

Of course, geologists present a much different explanation. Tens of millions of years ago, two of the earth's tectonic plates collided. It was not a sudden crash, but a slow, powerful push that has occurred over many, many years. The collision pushed the earth down and produced such heat that some of the earth's crust began to melt. As it cooled, this molten rock turned into granite.

As the two plates plowed into each other, granite and sedimentary rock were pushed upward.

This formed the Alaska Range, a six-hundred-mile (966-kilometer) mountain chain that includes Mt. McKinley. In subsequent millennia, erosion wore down the mountains. But because Mount McKinley was composed mostly of hard granite, its size diminished at a much lower rate than did mountains that were mostly comprised of sedimentary rock.

The Alaska Range is part of the Denali Fault system, the largest crustal break on the continent. This fault stretches for 1,300 miles (2,092 kilometers). Along this fault system, which separates the Alaska and Aleutian Ranges, are many mountain peaks. Earthquake tremors frequently occur in the area.

For tens of thousands of years, various ice ages affected the landscape. Mobile glaciers sculpted the land, carving rock and scooping out valleys. The last ice age ended about twelve thousand years ago. With the meltdown, vegetation returned to the northern climbs of the continent. Moreover, while most wooly mammoths died by 8,000 B.C., a population of them survived in Alaska as late as 6,000 B.C.

HUMANS DISCOVER THE GREAT MOUNTAIN

It is hard for us to comprehend, but humans have lived in the shadows of Denali for at least twelve thousand years. On the lowlands of the region,

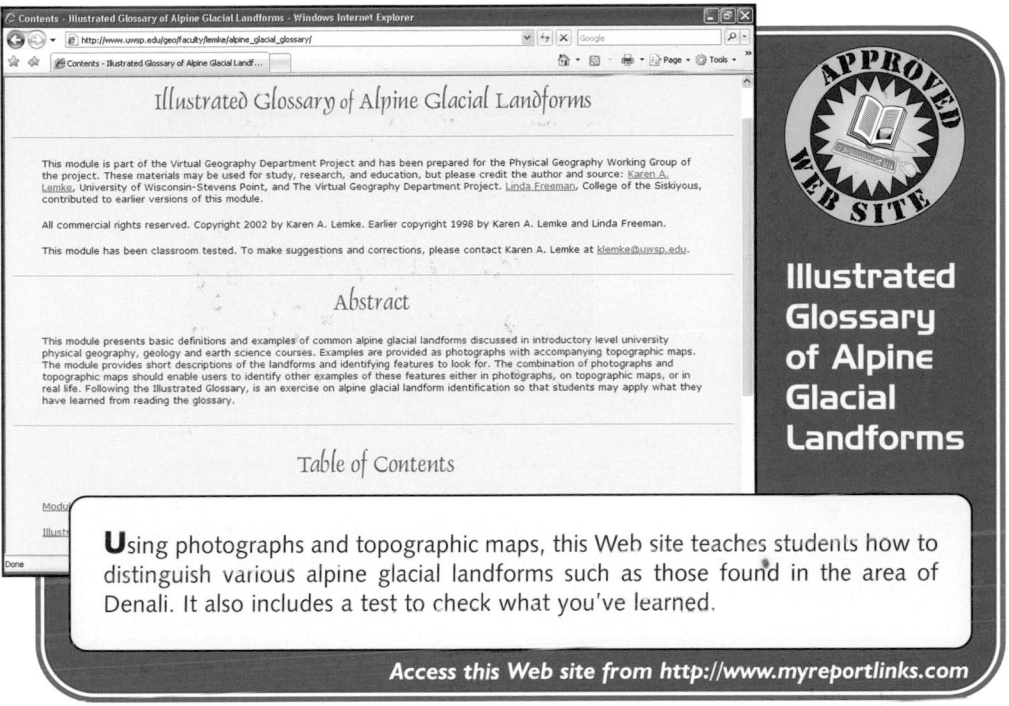

Illustrated Glossary of Alpine Glacial Landforms

Using photographs and topographic maps, this Web site teaches students how to distinguish various alpine glacial landforms such as those found in the area of Denali. It also includes a test to check what you've learned.

Access this Web site from http://www.myreportlinks.com

Athabascans hunted caribou, sheep, and moose. They also fished and foraged for berries and edible plants. During winters, they lived in sheltered areas in the valleys. Besides naming Denali, the Athabascans had a name for the second tallest mountain on the range: They called it Menlale, meaning Denali's wife.

Athabascan culture thrived all the way into the 1800s. As with other American Indian tribes, the arrival of white men triggered their demise. White traders, visitors, and settlers unintentionally transmitted diseases to which Athabascans were not immune. As a result, many of these natives died.

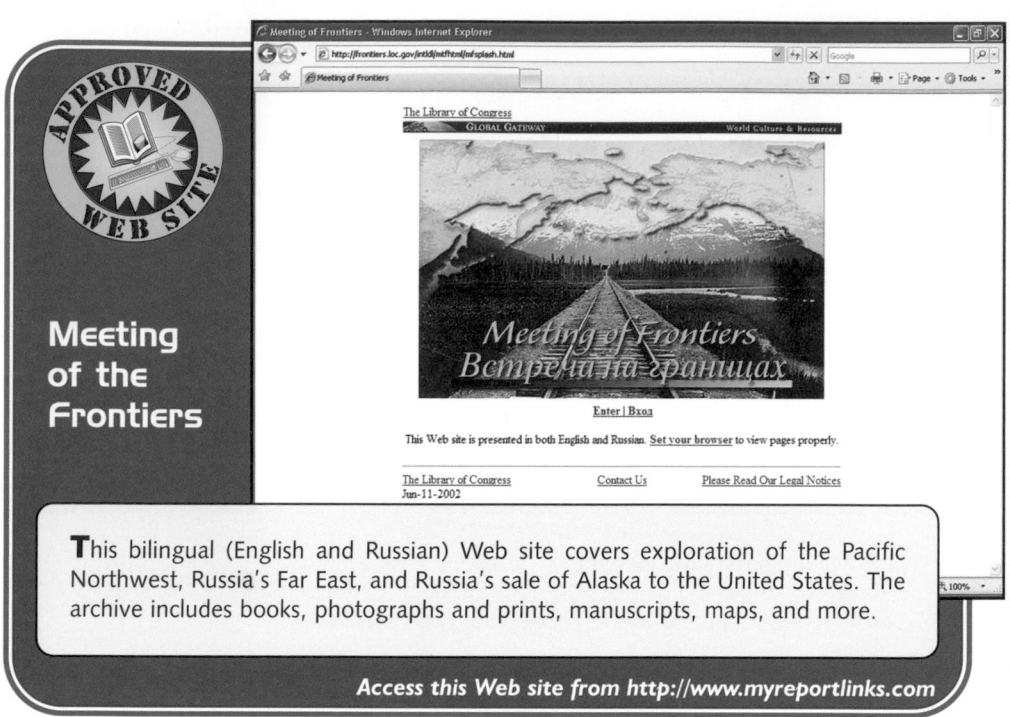

Meeting
of the
Frontiers

The Library of Congress
GLOBAL GATEWAY   World Culture & Resources

Meeting of Frontiers
Встреча на границах

Enter | Вход

This Web site is presented in both English and Russian. Set your browser to view pages properly.

The Library of Congress   Contact Us   Please Read Our Legal Notices
Jun-11-2002

This bilingual (English and Russian) Web site covers exploration of the Pacific Northwest, Russia's Far East, and Russia's sale of Alaska to the United States. The archive includes books, photographs and prints, manuscripts, maps, and more.

Access this Web site from http://www.myreportlinks.com

Although Europeans occupied North America for several hundred years, none of them knew about the highest point on the continent. It wasn't until 1794 that British explorer George Vancouver noted in his journal "distant stupendous mountains covered with snow, and apparently detached from each other."[1]

During much of the 1800s, Russians attempted to colonize the territory of Alaska. In 1867, they abandoned their efforts and sold Alaska to the United States. U.S. Secretary of State William Seward agreed on a price of $7.2 million. Many Americans thought he had overpaid for the frozen land. They even called the purchase "Seward's

Folly." Yet as American explorers and scientists got to know Alaska, they realized it was rich in beauty and natural resources. The purchase was not a folly but, in fact, the bargain of the century.

→ How Mt. McKinley Got Its Name

American Indians in Alaska—and even white Alaskans—have forever resented the name Mt. McKinley. The revered mountain had been called Denali for ages. It wasn't until 1896 that someone decided to call it something else. White prospector William A. Dickey named the mountain "after William McKinley of Ohio," he recalled, "who had been nominated for the presidency, and

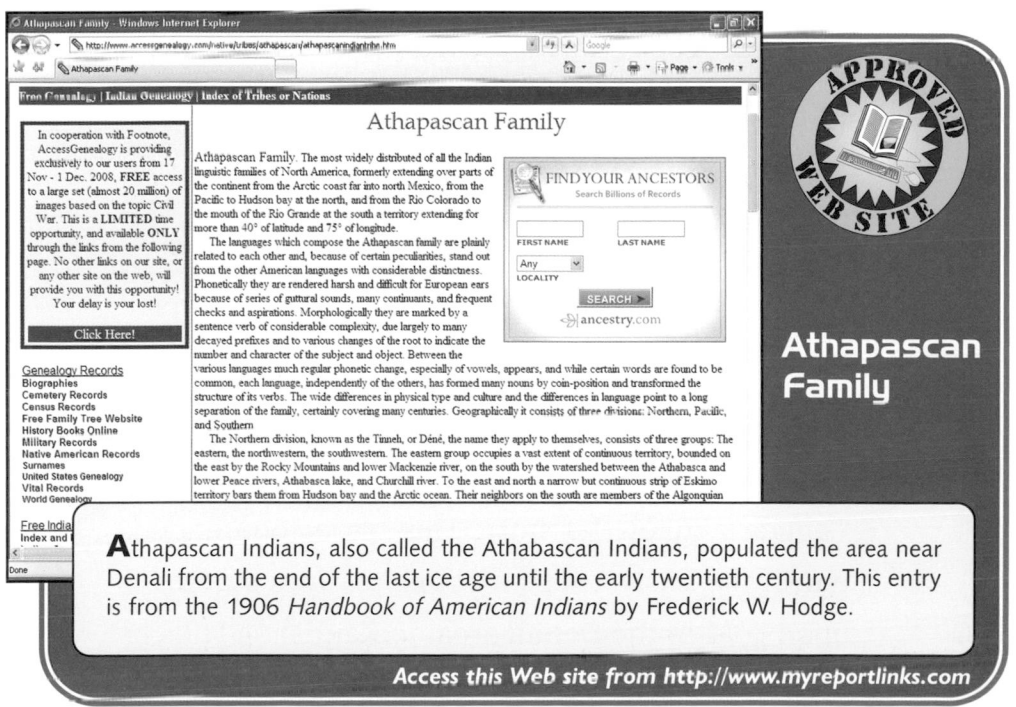

Athapascan Indians, also called the Athabascan Indians, populated the area near Denali from the end of the last ice age until the early twentieth century. This entry is from the 1906 *Handbook of American Indians* by Frederick W. Hodge.

Access this Web site from http://www.myreportlinks.com

that fact was the first news we received on our way out of that wonderful wilderness."[2]

The *New York Sun* reported Dickey's findings in its January 24, 1897, edition, and the name stuck. Two years later, explorer Joseph S. Herron named the region's second tallest mountain Mt. Foraker after U.S. Senator J. B. Foraker. This politician also hailed from Ohio, a state three thousand miles (4,828 kilometers) away.

Be it Denali or McKinley, mountaineers became obsessed with climbing the range's highest mountain. In 1902, Alfred Hulse Brooks became the first known person to set foot on Mt. McKinley's slopes. He ascended 7,500 feet (2,286 meters) before turning back. In 1903, Judge James Wickersham's party reached 8,000 feet (2,438 meters) and the Dr. Frederick A. Cook expedition made it to 11,000 feet (3,353 meters). But for years no one would come close to the mountaintop. In fact, the big news in the region at the time had nothing to do with Mt. McKinley.

⊜ GOLD IN THEM THERE HILLS

In the late 1890s a gold rush erupted in western Canada's Yukon Territory. This craze soon ended, but in the early 1900s a couple of Joes stumbled upon gold in the Denali area. In Kantishna Hills in 1904, Joseph Dalton prospected for the precious

Woolly Mammoth - Learning Adventures - Windows Internet Explorer

http://school.discoveryeducation.com/schooladventures/woollymammoth/

Woolly Mammoth - Learning Adventures

Educator Login | Passcode Login

Discovery EDUCATION

Products & Services | Classroom Resources | Home Resources | Professional Development | Store

PUZZLEMAKER | LESSON PLAN LIBRARY | KATHY SCHROCK'S GUIDE | FUN TOOLS ▼ | SCIENCE FAIR CENTRAL | NEW TEACHER | CONTESTS & GRANTS ▼

Classroom Resources > Learning Adventures

Search Classroom Resources: [search] **GO**

○ Science

WOOLLY MAMMOTH

After battling weeks of bad weather and 20,000 years worth of permafrost, scientists in Siberia have done the unthinkable—excavated a 20,380 year-old woolly mammoth in hopes of cloning these Ice Age giants.

Impossible? Perhaps. But just in case the Pleistocene Epoch makes a comeback, you'd better be prepared. First, test your Ice Age I.Q. by playing **Seven Steppes to a Woollier Mammoth.** Then head to the **Mammoth Migration Map** and follow the evolution of our furry friends.

You can also still click on **Join the Expedition** to read archived reports from the big Siberian dig.

If you think finding fossils under 20,000 years of ice is hard, try to navigate the **woolly mammoth maze** in Puzzlemaker.

Home | Seven Steppes to a Woollier Mammoth | Woolly Web Links | Join the Expedition

★ Related Materials

China Rises 4-Pack DVD

Product Type: DVD
Price: 219.95

China is emerging as a preeminent superpower of the 21st Century. How does a country with thousands of years of tradition transfol...

Visit the Teacherstore ▶

NEW TEACHER survival CENTRAL

Get tech ti homeroom the best of the

APPROVED WEB SITE

Wooly mammoths began to decline around 10,000 B.C., but the species survived in Alaska for about another four thousand years. This Discovery Channel Web page called **Wooly Mammoth** presents an activity covering the species' evolution, a map of its migration to Alaska, and more.

---

metal in a river basin. In 1905, Joe Quigley found gold in Glacier Creek.

Upon hearing the news, many out-of-work gold prospectors from the Yukon rushed to Kantishna. Within weeks, thousands arrived to mine the Tanana, Bearpaw, and Kantishna rivers. These men hastily constructed mining towns, including Eureka (a word miners used when they struck gold). Sadly for the hopeful miners, not much gold was available to excavate. After six months, with the gold mostly gone, nearly everyone left. Workers in the area were able to mine silver, lead,

Charles Sheldon was drawn in by the breathtaking views that Denali has to offer. It inspired him to push for Denali to become a national park.

and zinc. However, a lack of roads limited their effectiveness. The mining craze died, and those in the region turned their attention to other pursuits.

➡ PRESERVING THE BEAUTY

In the late 1800s a conservationist movement swept North America. Thanks to railroads, more and more people became aware of the awesome beauty of the American West. They feared that industrialists would exploit the resources, and that hunters would decimate big-game populations. Conservationists sought to protect the land, and they had plenty of supporters in Washington. In 1872, President Ulysses S. Grant signed a bill that made Yellowstone the world's first national park.

John Muir preached about the importance of preserving America's beauty, and the nation listened. By 1906 the federal government had established seven national parks in the West, stretching from Colorado to California. But what about Alaska? The champion for an Alaskan national park came from an unlikely place—even farther away than Ohio.

An East Coast gentleman, Charles Sheldon looked dapper in his three-piece suits. Yet Sheldon had grown up near the mountains of Vermont, and he loved the great outdoors. He became a member of New York's Boone and Crockett Club, and in 1906 he made an ambitious excursion to the

Mountaineering - Windows Internet Explorer

http://www.nps.gov/archive/dena/home/mountaineering/history.htm

Mountaineering

National Park Service

National Park Service
U.S. Department of the Interior

Mountaineering

Denali National Park and Preserve
Alaska

CLIMBING HISTORY

Mountaineering Homepage
Mountaineering Booklet
Registration & Permits
Summary Reports
Current Weather Conditions / Statistics
Area Services
Climbing History
Clean Mountain Cans

From leather boots and canvas packs, climbing on Denali has changed through the years. NPS photos

Weather »
Current weather conditions on the mountain.

Although Mt. McKinley can be seen from Anchorage on a clear day, its base is deep in the Alaska Range. Explorers in the early 1900s used river boats, mules, and dog sleds to gain access to the mountain's glaciers in order to establish base camps.

Through timeline entries dating from 1794 to 2004, the **Denali Climbing History** Web page describes milestones in climbing Denali, or Mount McKinley. Links on the page provide information for interested climbers, covering registration, transportation and support services, and authorized guides.

Alaskan wilderness. His intention was to study the region's mountain sheep, but he quickly became enamored with all that he saw.

Sheldon drew sketches of his surroundings, and in his journal did his best to capture the sights and sounds. "A chickadee flitted among the upper-most willows. . . ," he wrote. "Great avalanches continually kept falling with crashing sounds that rolled among the outside ranges."[3]

Most of all, Sheldon fell under the spell of Mt. McKinley. "The great mountain rose above me desolate, magnificent, overpowering," he wrote.

"The lower ranges were white, while below, nothing could be seen but the fog, which took on the appearance of thick clouds. I felt, as never before, completely alone in the presence of this mighty mountain; no words can describe my feelings."[4]

Sheldon believed that the area surrounding Mt. McKinley should be designated a national

park. Previously, few had contemplated such a notion. After all, most of Alaska was untamed wilderness, and the McKinley region was not in danger of exploitation. But Sheldon was a man on a mission.

In 1907, he traveled back to Alaska with a guide named Harry Karstens. Sheldon spent much of his ten-month stay studying potential boundaries for his proposed park. When he returned east, he convinced the Boone and Crockett Club to campaign for a national park that would surround Mt. McKinley. The club's influential members supported the idea, but it would take nearly a decade for Sheldon's dream to come true.

➲ TO THE MOUNTAINTOP

On September 27, 1906, mountain climber Dr. Frederick A. Cook sent a startling telegram. After just two short weeks, he stated, he and a fellow climber had reached the summit of

◀ *Mountain climbers continue to be challenged by Denali's dangerous peaks such as High Rock Cliff, shown here.*

Mt. McKinley. The achievement seemed hard to believe, and sure enough Cook had lied. In his 1908 book, *To the Top of the Continent,* he included a photograph of—supposedly—the summit of Mt. McKinley. But other climbers later proved that the photo was fraudulent. The "Fake Peak" was only a quarter way up the mountain, at 5,300 feet (1,615 meters).

In 1910, climbers Thomas Lloyd, Charlie McGonagall, Billy Taylor, and Pete Anderson made a valiant effort to reach the top of Mt. McKinley. Subsisting on donuts and hot cocoa during their final hours of climbing, Taylor and Anderson made it to the top of the North Peak. It wasn't the

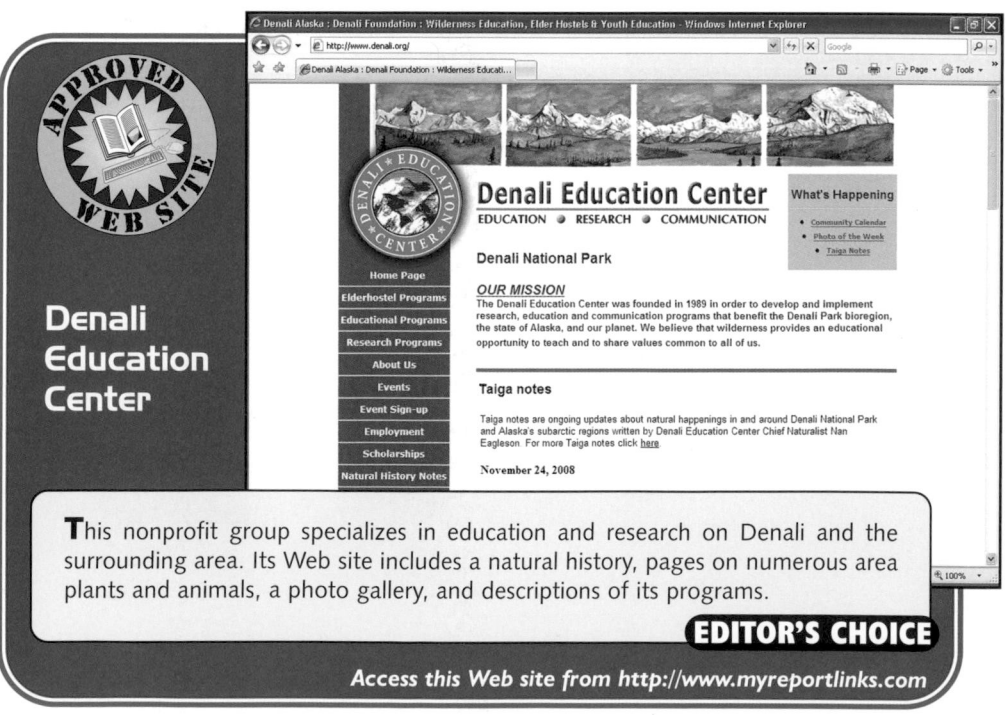

Denali Education Center

This nonprofit group specializes in education and research on Denali and the surrounding area. Its Web site includes a natural history, pages on numerous area plants and animals, a photo gallery, and descriptions of its programs.

EDITOR'S CHOICE

Access this Web site from http://www.myreportlinks.com

mountain's summit, but it was 19,470 feet (5,934 meters) high—an extraordinary achievement.

In 1912 two more parties attempted to conquer the giant mountain. One group from Fairbanks, Alaska, reached eight thousand feet (2,438 meters) before storms forced their retreat. Another party, led by popular artist Belmore Browne, climbed to within a hundred vertical yards (91.4 meters) of the summit. Yet bad weather made their final ascent impossible.

The next year, the Stuck party became the first to reach the summit of Mt. McKinley (see Chapter 1). The men had climbed more than twenty thousand feet (6,096 meters) of rock, much of which was encased in slippery snow and ice. Temperatures had plunged to –30°F (–34°C). And yet, Stuck noted, "Not a single mishap had occurred to mar the complete success of our undertaking—not a single injury of any sort to any one. . . . All five of us were in perfect health."[5]

Once Mt. McKinley was conquered, people were no longer interested in climbing it. If you're not going to be the first, they reasoned, it's not worth the agony. A full nineteen years passed before another group of climbers tried to conquer Mt. McKinley.

SHELDON PUSHES FOR A PARK

After the Stuck party's historic climb, Charles Sheldon became the region's greatest champion.

He continued his campaign to make the Mount McKinley region a national park. McKinley climbers Belmore Brown and James Wickersham joined him in his efforts.

The National Park Service's official Denali Web site notes that in Alaska, "[m]ajestic mountains were not hard to come by. But here, just north of the Alaska Range, one could find a region with [a] magic combination of wildlife and scenery that typified the territory."[6]

GETTING HELP IN WASHINGTON

Sheldon noted that if the McKinley region wasn't protected soon, human activity would ruin it. Miners were all over the region, digging for valuable minerals. In 1915 construction began on a railroad that would link the nearby town of Fairbanks to Alaska's southern coast. This was a bad omen for the wild game that lived just north of the Alaska Range. Hunters would undoubtedly kill these animals to feed railway workers and communities that would grow near the completed railroad. Sheldon was particularly concerned with the Dall sheep of the region.

Sheldon found plenty of sympathizers in Washington, D.C. During the mid- to late 1910s, Congress was more inclined than ever before to designate land as a national park. In 1916, for the first time, three American regions were so honored.

Then, on February 19, 1917, Congress passed a bill creating Mt. McKinley National Park (N.P.). Two million acres were set aside as a wildlife preserve.

Fittingly, Sheldon had the honor of delivering the bill personally to President Woodrow Wilson. On February 26, 1917, the president signed the bill into law—and gave the pen to Sheldon.

Chapter 3

Building roads to Denali was one of the challenges facing supporters of the park when it opened in 1917.

Alaska's National Park

While Alaskans were proud of their first national park, they were disappointed with the name. They had hoped that it would be proclaimed Denali National Park, after the natives' original name for the mountain. But the powers in Washington preferred the "patriotic" McKinley, in honor of the twenty-fifth president.

At least most everyone was happy with the park's first superintendent. Harry Karstens had first come to the region during the Klondike gold rush in the late 1890s. He had also helped Sheldon as a packer and guide during Sheldon's first trips to the Denali area.

As superintendent, Karstens immediately faced a major problem. Men were ignoring the fact that animals in the new national park were off-limits to hunters. Poachers (those who hunt illegally) were killing Dall sheep and other animals and

selling the meat to miners and railroad workers.
Karstens and his park rangers took action. They
formed multiple dogsled patrols, even building
the sleds and training the dogs themselves. These
patrols guarded the park's boundaries and
enforced the no-hunting regulations. Poachers
soon got the message. They left the park and took
their hunting elsewhere.

A Park Without Visitors

The Denali park headquarters, originally stationed
in Nenana, Alaska, moved to the Riley Creek area
in 1922. Yet hardly anyone even noticed. In the
early years of the park, tourism was almost nonex-
istent. When the Savage Tourist Camp was
established in 1923, only thirty-four visitors took
advantage of it that season.

It's not that people didn't want to go to the
new park. The problem was how to get there.
Eventually, transportation to the Denali region
improved. In the summer of 1923, workers completed the Alaska Railroad. It stretched from
nearby Fairbanks to Seward on the southern
Alaska coast. It also made the park easily accessible from both Fairbanks and Anchorage. President
Warren G. Harding traveled across the continent
to attend the ceremony. While he was in the
neighborhood, he became the first president to
visit Mt. McKinley National Park.

Alaska's Digital Archives : Home - Windows Internet Explorer

http://vilda.alaska.edu/index.php

Alaska's Digital Archives : Home

Alaska's Digital Archives

Help   About   Preferences   FAQs

Search

Advanced Search

Browse

My Favorites

SLED
Statewide Library Electronic Doorway

Alaska's Digital Archives presents a wealth of historical photographs, albums, oral histories, moving images, maps, documents, physical objects, and other materials from libraries, museums and archives throughout our state.

Alaska Native History & Cultures

Movement to Statehood

The land now known as the state of Alaska has been continuously inhabited by Native peoples for thousands of years. We invite you to view images of the indigenous people of our state. GO »

The United States acquired Ala_ in 1867. The territory became t 49th state in 1959. These imag document people, events and places in Alaska from the 1860s through the early years of statehood. GO »

100%

Alaska's Digital Archives stores over ten thousand items covering Alaska's native history & culture and the movement to statehood. Presented are historical photographs, moving images, maps, documents, and photographs of physical objects.

Meanwhile, construction crews worked on a park road. Due to the rugged terrain, the roadway took years to complete. They finished twelve miles (19.3 kilometers) of road by 1924 and forty miles (64.4 kilometers) by 1928. But even in 1928—the pinnacle of the prosperous Roaring '20s—fewer than five hundred people visited the park. By comparison, Yellowstone National Park welcomed a record 230,000 tourists that year.

In the 1930s the Great Depression gripped North America. Ironically, the economic crisis benefited the national parks. President Franklin

Roosevelt created the Civilian Conservation Corps (CCC), which put 3 million people to work on outdoor projects. Many of them labored at national parks, including Mt. McKinley.

Throughout the 1930s construction boomed at the Alaskan park. Workers constructed an airstrip near the post office and train depot. They also extended the road to Wonder Lake and built a ranger station near its shore. In addition, CCC workers constructed the McKinley Park Station Hotel. They built the hotel for the Alaska Railroad, and it became the lodging of choice for park visitors.

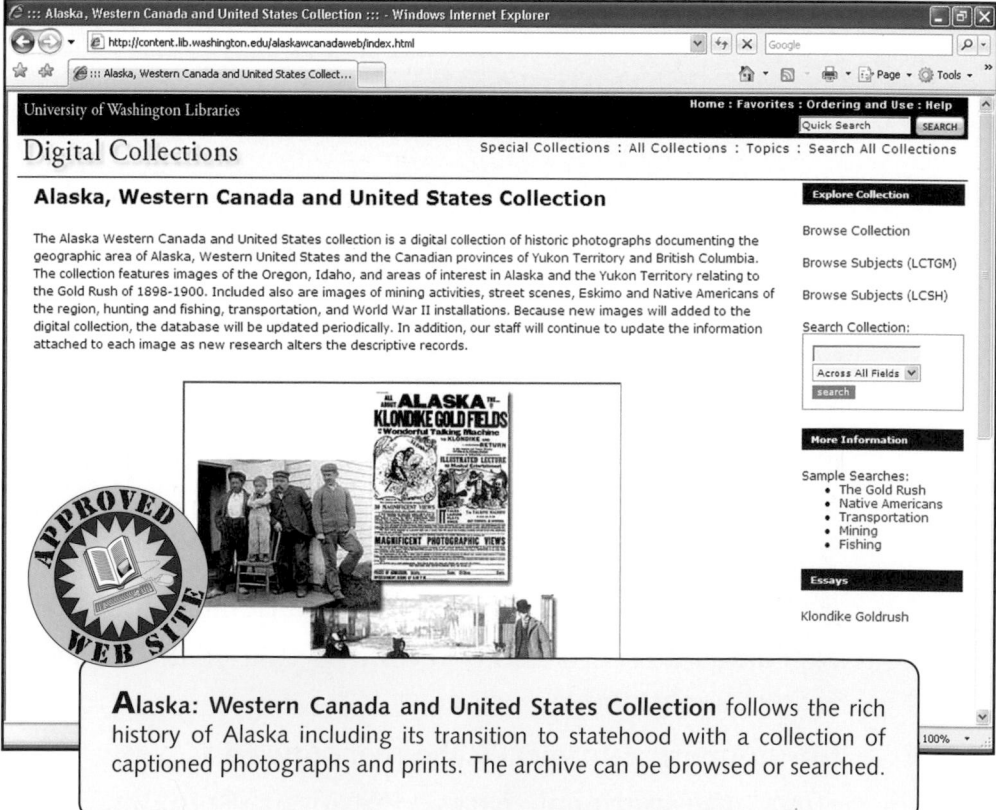

Alaska: **Western Canada and United States Collection** follows the rich history of Alaska including its transition to statehood with a collection of captioned photographs and prints. The archive can be browsed or searched.

Unfortunately, many of the hotel guests disliked their view. They complained that it was impossible to see Mt. McKinley from anywhere in the hotel area. Apparently, the hotel needed to be next to the railroad, and the railroad couldn't be built near the mountain because of rocky terrain. The hotel's disappointing views contributed to the park's continued low attendance.

So, too, did the onset of the Second World War. In 1942 the park welcomed fewer than one hundred visitors to its 2 million acres (809,371 hectares). However, U.S. Army personnel made good use of the park. They used the site to test cold-weather clothing and equipment. They also utilized it as a military recreation camp for those troops stationed in Alaska. Climbing Mt. McKinley was not on their list of fun activities. But after the war, numerous climbers attempted to summit the High One just for the thrill of it.

EXTRAORDINARY CLIMBS

While no one attempted to reach Mt. McKinley's summit from 1914 to 1932, many thousands have tried since. Moreover, close to a hundred people have died trying. On June 6, 1947, Barbara Washburn made history by becoming the first woman to reach the top of Mt. McKinley.

Over the years, certain men, women, and children have made noteworthy climbs. Incredibly, eleven-year-old boy Galen Johnston reached the top of the monolith in 2001. Merrick Johnston, age twelve, became the youngest girl to do so in 1995. Ten years later, seventy-four-year-old Sadao Hoshiko became the oldest person to climb to the top.

Ray Genet set the record for the most successful climbs to the summit—twenty-seven. Japanese adventurer Naomi Uemura twice entered the record books. He was the first to reach the top solo (in 1970) and the first to climb to the summit in winter (1984). Tragically, he died on the descent.

Alaska Wildlife Alliance is a nonprofit group supporting Alaskan wildlife. Its Web site describes its campaigns to help preserve wolves, wolverines, bears, marine mammals, and their habitat. The site includes photographs and video presentations on some of its campaigns.

Four other extraordinary climbers deserve mention. Sarah Doherty in 1985 became the first to make the ascent with a missing leg and no artificial limb. In 1999, Ed Hommer reached the summit despite missing both legs. In 1993, Joan Phelps conquered the mountain despite being blind. And on June 16, 1997, Michael Rilenge became the first person with muscular dystrophy to make it to the top of Mt. McKinley.

➔ THE WOLVES AND ADOLPH MURIE

In the 1940s the National Park Service struggled with the question of wolf control. For years, officials at multiple national parks allowed the extermination of wolves because the canines supposedly were killing too many big-game animals. But over time, many ecologists began to doubt this policy. They argued that humans should not interfere with the natural ecosystem. By eliminating a predator like the wolf, they reasoned, the size of another animal population might grow too large and affect the population of other animals. It's best, they said, to let nature take its course.

In the 1940s the debate over the wolves raged in Mt. McKinley N.P. Many worried about the drastic decline in the treasured Dall sheep. Especially severe winters and predators (the wolves), caused this. Biologist Adolph Murie was asked to study the situation, and in 1944 he released a

▲ *A moose crosses Wonder Lake. At one time, a hotel was nearly built along Wonder Lake, but the wilderness surrounding the lake has remained pristine.*

landmark book, *The Wolves of Mt. McKinley*. Murie revealed that the wolves actually were not deci- mating the Dall sheep population. They preyed only on the sick, old, and weak sheep, which in a sense strengthened the sheep herd. The National Park Service maintained a limited amount of wolf control in its parks into the 1950s. However, Murie's book fueled a movement to end the practice for good.

Like Charles Sheldon, Murie proved to be a great champion of the Denali region. He believed in preserving not just the area's wildlife but its entire ecosystem. At other national parks, thousands of tourists roared through the gates in their automobiles. They shattered nature's delicate makeup with noise, fumes, and the foreign microorganisms on the bottoms of their shoes. As Mt. McKinley's resident biologist, Murie strongly insisted that his park not become a Yellowstone-type playground.

The National Park Service proposed building a hotel at Wonder Lake and widening and paving the park road. But due largely to Murie's influence, the hotel was never built and the primitive road remained untouched. To this day, the park's ecosystem remains intact, its wilderness in an almost pristine condition.

➡ TOURISTS FLOCK TO DENALI

Following World War II, the American tourism industry boomed. After fifteen years of economic depression and war, Americans had the money, desire, and means (automobiles) to explore their country. Yet at Mt. McKinley National Park, annual attendance remained low. Even as late as 1956 it stood at a meager five thousand. However, the completion of the Denali Highway in 1957 finally brought the tourists. Vacationers could take the smooth roadway all the way to the park entrance. In 1958 attendance skyrocketed to twenty-five thousand.

Alaska, an American territory for nearly a century, became a state in 1959. Nine years later, another major event occurred in Alaska: The Atlantic-Richfield Company discovered oil at Prudhoe Bay. With Alaska's land suddenly valuable, debates raged about who was entitled to its riches—the U.S. government or the natives who had lived on the land for centuries? In 1971 the

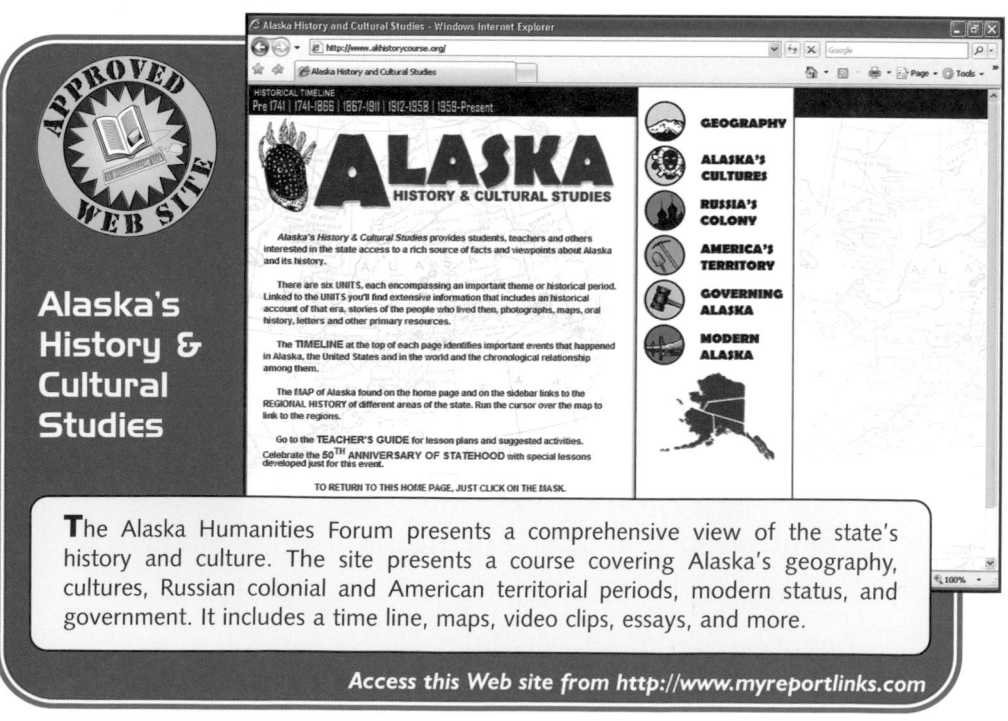

Alaska's History & Cultural Studies

The Alaska Humanities Forum presents a comprehensive view of the state's history and culture. The site presents a course covering Alaska's geography, cultures, Russian colonial and American territorial periods, modern status, and government. It includes a time line, maps, video clips, essays, and more.

Access this Web site from http://www.myreportlinks.com

two sides struck a deal. Alaskan Natives would relinquish claims to the land, and as compensation they would receive 44 million designated acres and nearly $1 billion. American industry was free to drill for oil—billions of dollars' worth.

While oil-company workers poured into Alaska, tourists began flocking to Mt. McKinley National Park. The big breakthrough was the completion of the George Parks Highway in 1972. This major road linked the park to Anchorage and Fairbanks, Alaska's two largest cities. As a result, park attendance doubled from 44,528 in 1971 to 88,615 in 1972. For years afterward, attendance figures continued to soar.

⮕ Many Come to Climb

So, too, did the number of climbers on Mt. McKinley. In 1976 a record 508 climbers attempted to conquer the mountain. Enlisting the help of experienced guides, many of the adventurers were successful. In fact, on July 6, 1976, eighty climbers reached the summit of Mt. McKinley. This is not to say that it was easy. That same year, two of the world's most famous climbers, Doug Scott and Dougal Haston, struggled up Mt. McKinley. "We were drawing heavily on all our Himalayan experience just to survive," they admitted, "and it was a respectful pair that finally stood on the summit ridge. Everything was cold, even our souls."[1]

Also in 1976, the United Nations honored the park by selecting it as a world biosphere reserve. Such reserves were created "to promote and demonstrate a balanced relationship between humans and the biosphere." After decades of obscurity, this national park was making a name for itself. In 1980 its name would change altogether.[2]

FROM MCKINLEY TO DENALI

December 2, 1980, was monumental for the state of Alaska. That day, outgoing president Jimmy Carter signed the Alaska National Interest Lands Conservation Act. The new law provided for the designation of 79.54 million acres (32.19 million hectares) of Alaskan land. With the stroke of a pen, the number of national parks in Alaska jumped from one to eight.

Moreover, the new law called for the expansion of Mt. McKinley National Park—from 2 million acres (809,371 hectares) to 6 million (2.4 million hectares). With the new boundaries, the park included all of Mt. McKinley and the glaciers on the south side of the Alaska Range. The park was also expanded to the west and north to accommodate the region's entire caribou herd. The expansion thus fulfilled Adolph Murie's dream of fully protecting the region's ecosystem.

Congress also honored the wishes of deceased park pioneer Charles Sheldon—as well as most

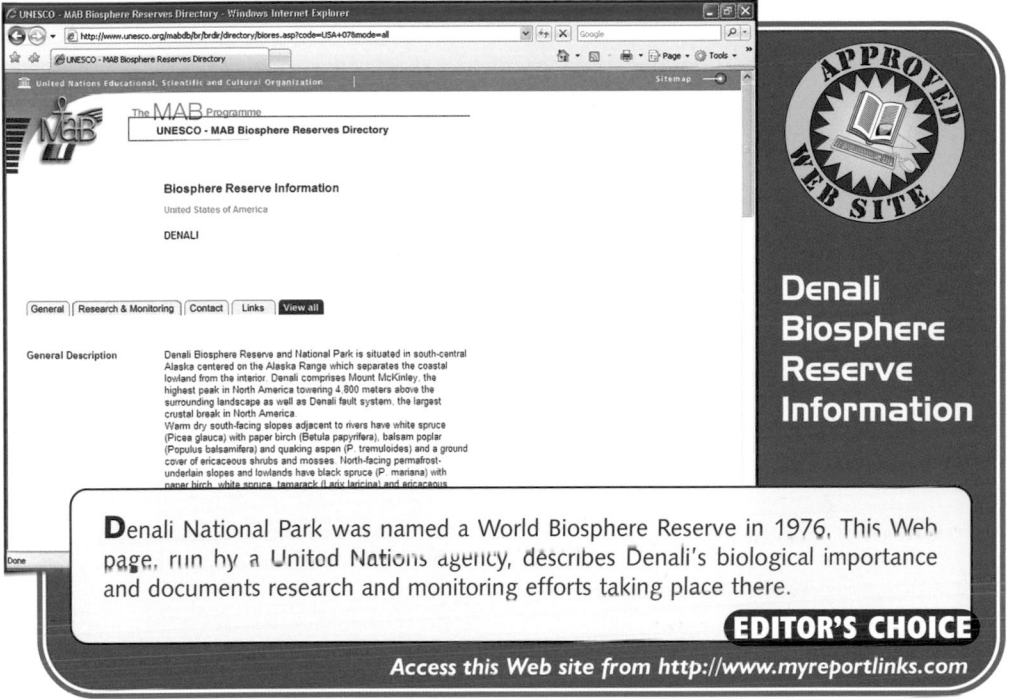

Denali National Park was named a World Biosphere Reserve in 1976. This Web page, run by a United Nations agency, describes Denali's biological importance and documents research and monitoring efforts taking place there.

EDITOR'S CHOICE

Access this Web site from http://www.myreportlinks.com

Alaskans. It changed the name of Mt. McKinley National Park to Denali National Park & Preserve.

Congress also sectioned off the park. Denali NP&P's 6 million acres included the Denali Wilderness—the 2 million acres that formerly comprised the old park. The Denali Preserve constituted lands to the west of the original park. (A national preserve is federally protected land. However, certain activities not permitted in a national park may be allowed in a preserve, such as hunting and oil extraction.)

Meanwhile, the name of the mountain became the subject of hot debate. Around the time of the renaming of the park, the Alaska Board of

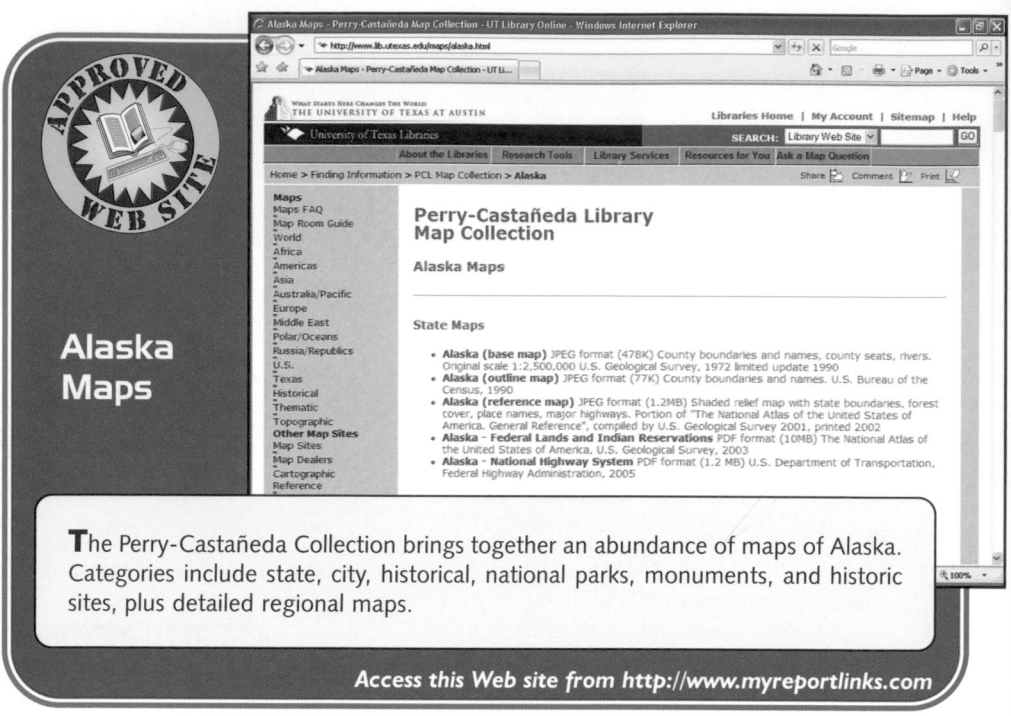

The Perry-Castañeda Collection brings together an abundance of maps of Alaska. Categories include state, city, historical, national parks, monuments, and historic sites, plus detailed regional maps.

Access this Web site from http://www.myreportlinks.com

Geographic Names changed the name of the mountain to Denali. However, the U.S. Board of Geographic Names continued to call it McKinley. To this day, both boards have stuck to their decisions.

⊜ BUSES AND CLIMBERS

During the 1980s, Denali NP&P became a mecca for nature lovers and adventurers. In 1987 more than 570,000 visitors enjoyed the splendor of the park and preserve. Yet unlike other national parks, Denali avoided the pollution of thousands of automobiles. Upon arrival, visitors hopped on park shuttle buses, which transported them to their destination of choice. Meanwhile, the number of mountain climbers continued to soar, topping one thousand for the first time in 1989.

Of course, in the heart of the cold, untamed wilderness, danger was ever-present. In 1992 eleven climbers died on Mt. McKinley due to severe storms and extreme cold. Two others perished on Mt. Foraker that year. The tragedy rekindled the issue about unqualified climbers attempting to ascend Mt. McKinley. They put not only their own lives in danger but those of rescue workers as well. Beginning in 1995, aspiring climbers were required to obtain a permit to ascend McKinley, which included a fee that is currently $200. Permit or not, climbers continued to flock to the mountain by the hundreds.

Chapter

4

A grizzly bear takes a stroll through Denali National Park and Preserve during the scenic autumn months.

The Wild Life

Denali is not the largest national park in the United States. That distinction belongs to Alaska's Wrangell-St. Elias National Park & Preserve. Yet Denali is so vast, and its mountains so tall, it seems like an entire world unto itself.

Mt. McKinley is not only the tallest mountain in North America, but its summit is higher than that of any in the world except for those in the Himalayas (Asia) and the Andes (South America). Denali also features numerous other colossal mountains as well as many enormous glaciers. And yet the park and preserve feature far more than rock and ice. Denali's 6 million-plus acres (2,428,114 hectares) contain a complete ecosystem with a rich variety of plants and animals.

➡ PEAKS AND VALLEYS

Mt. McKinley is the pinnacle of the great Alaska Range, which slices through the park from east to west. This six-hundred-mile (966-kilometer) mountain range is an important natural barrier in southern Alaska. To the south of the range lie coastal lowlands, which include the state's largest city, Anchorage. On the western side of the range, rivers flow south to the Gulf of Alaska and west to the Bering Sea.

The Alaska Range strides along the 1,300-mile (2,092-kilometer) Denali Fault, the longest crustal break in North America. The fault causes frequent earthquake tremors in the park, although very few are even felt by the area's residents.

⊜ICE AND WATER

Within Denali NP& P, the Alaska Range's elevation generally fluctuates between 7,000 and 9,000 feet (2,134 and 2,743 meters). Mt. McKinley (20,320 feet (6,194 meters)) and Mt. Foraker (17,400 feet (5,304 meters)) are notable exceptions. But not all of Denali is up in the clouds. To the north of the Alaska Range rests Wonder Lake, which sits only 2,000 feet (610 meters) above sea level. The elevation difference between this lake and Mount McKinley's peak—more than 18,000 feet (5,486 meters)—is the largest in the world. Thus, it is not just mountains but the extreme variations in terrain that make Denali one of the most extraordinary geological regions on earth.

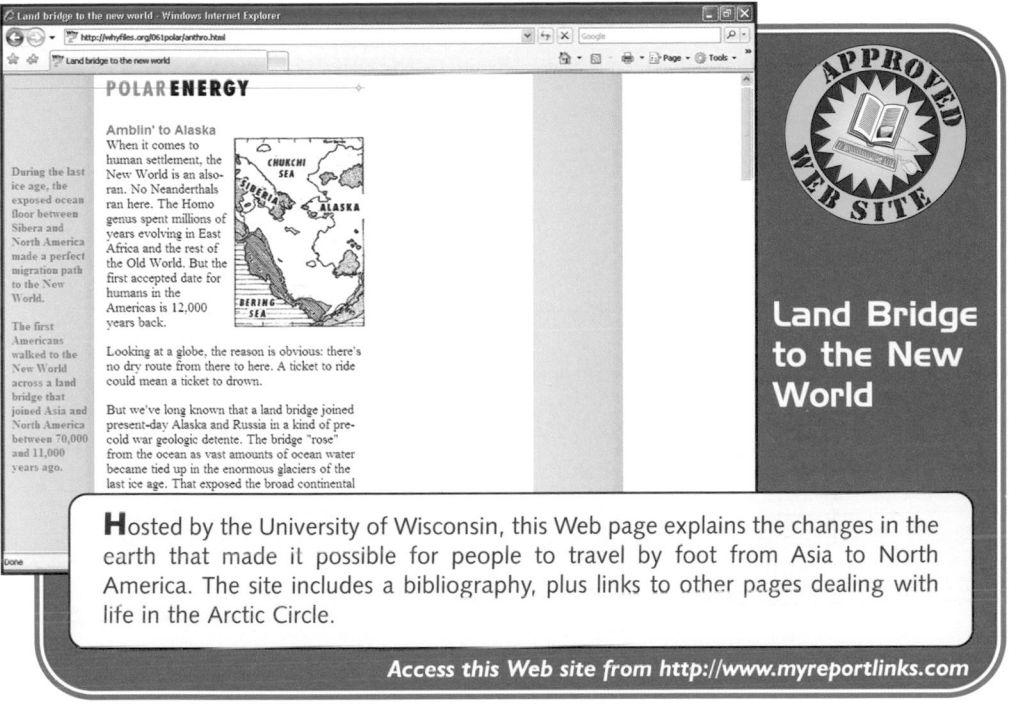

POLAR ENERGY

Amblin' to Alaska
When it comes to human settlement, the New World is an also-ran. No Neanderthals ran here. The Homo genus spent millions of years evolving in East Africa and the rest of the Old World. But the first accepted date for humans in the Americas is 12,000 years back.

Looking at a globe, the reason is obvious: there's no dry route from there to here. A ticket to ride could mean a ticket to drown.

But we've long known that a land bridge joined present-day Alaska and Russia in a kind of pre-cold war geologic detente. The bridge "rose" from the ocean as vast amounts of ocean water became tied up in the enormous glaciers of the last ice age. That exposed the broad continental

During the last ice age, the exposed ocean floor between Sibera and North America made a perfect migration path to the New World.

The first Americans walked to the New World across a land bridge that joined Asia and North America between 70,000 and 11,000 years ago.

Land Bridge to the New World

Hosted by the University of Wisconsin, this Web page explains the changes in the earth that made it possible for people to travel by foot from Asia to North America. The site includes a bibliography, plus links to other pages dealing with life in the Arctic Circle.

Access this Web site from http://www.myreportlinks.com

Over the millennia, glaciers have sculpted Denali's land. In fact, twenty massive glaciers still exist. Much of Denali is perpetually encased in ice, as glaciers cover 17 percent of the land. Kahiltna, Ruth, Eldridge, Tokositna, and Yentna are the largest of the glaciers. Located on the south side of the Alaska Range, these massive hunks of ice measure thirty-five to forty-five miles (56.3 to 72.4 kilometers) long. Glaciers are, technically, sliding pieces of ice, but they move at a snail's pace. The Ruth glacier, for instance, moves about three feet (0.9 meters) per day.

Water from the glaciers has filled up the park's crevices, leading to large rivers and numerous lakes and ponds. Wonder Lake is Denali's most famous body of water. It earned its name, according to legend, when a miner mused, "I wonder why we didn't notice this lake before."[1] If you drop a heavy item into Wonder Lake, you can kiss it goodbye: It's 268 feet (81.7 meters) to the bottom. The Chilchukabena Lake is just as long as Wonder Lake [2.6 miles (4.2 kilometers] but four times wider [two miles (3.2 kilometers)]. All told, the park and preserve contain 12,130 lakes and ponds and 18,679 miles (30,061 kilometers) of streams.

TAIGA AND TUNDRA

Although we tend to equate national parks with trees, only a fraction of Denali NP&P is wooded. But even in the wooded areas, known as taiga, trees do not actually flourish. In fact, *taiga* is a Russian word that means "land of little sticks."

The climate is so cold and harsh that taiga exists mostly in valleys near the rivers—where it is warmer and wetter. White spruce and black spruce (each of which would make good Christmas trees) dominate these areas. The quaking aspen, with its skinny white trunk, and the leafy balsam poplar also grow in these areas. In wooded sections, mosses and lichens often blanket the ground. In open areas, shrubs—such as blueberry and dwarf birch—dot the landscape. Because of

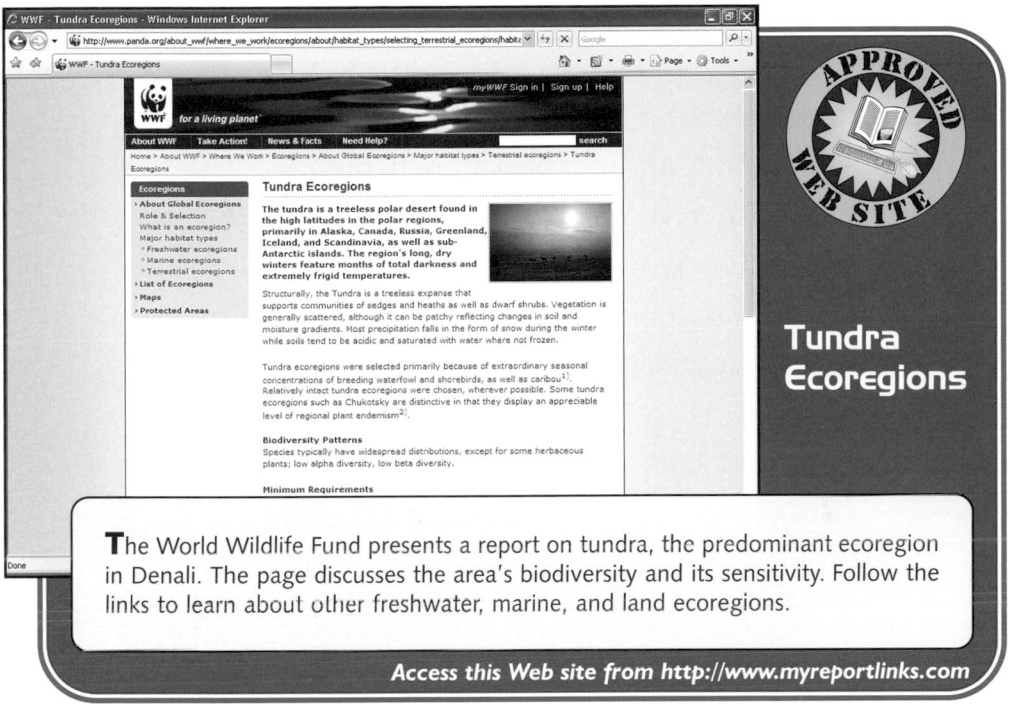

Tundra Ecoregions

The World Wildlife Fund presents a report on tundra, the predominant ecoregion in Denali. The page discusses the area's biodiversity and its sensitivity. Follow the links to learn about other freshwater, marine, and land ecoregions.

Access this Web site from http://www.myreportlinks.com

the cold weather and poor soil, most trees and bushes never reach full size.

While taiga covers some of Denali NP&P, tundra is the predominant terrain. Tundra is treeless land that is characteristic of the world's arctic and sub-arctic regions. It is located in high elevation, where the air is extremely cold. However, in places where topsoil covers the rock of the mountain, some hardy plant life thrives during the summer months. Grasses, mosses, ferns, and dwarfed shrubs all grow on this soil. In the "moist tundra," which is only partway up the mountains, blueberry and soapberry bushes flourish. Grizzly bears gobble these berries throughout the summer.

Up in the higher elevations, in the "dry tundra," some smaller plants are able to grow. In fact, a spectacular array of flowers decorates the mountains during the summer months. The for-get-me-not is one such flower. It has five flat, connected petals whose color is a shade of blue. Alaskan schoolchildren make sure they do not forget the forget-me-not. It is the official state flower.

More than 430 flowering plants can be found at Denali, although they bloom at different times. The appearance of the purple pasque flower signals the beginning of spring. Conversely, when the

Denali: Alaska's Great Wilderness, a companion site to a PBS program, spotlights the changes that occur in Denali between seasons. It features educational activities to help you understand permafrost, natural life found in Denali, and its weather.

EDITOR'S CHOICE

pink fireweed flowers finally bloom, summer is pretty much over.

Above the tundra life does not exist. In the upper elevations, you'll find nothing more than rock and—for much of the year, at least—ice and snow.

→ CHILLED TO THE BONE

You walk outside and it's chilly, cloudy, and damp. Though it's the middle of the afternoon, you need a warm jacket. After dinner, you notice a few flakes falling from the sky. It is not March, April, or even the end of autumn. It is Alaska, and it's the *middle of July.*

Even in Denali, on the southern end of the massive state, snow occasionally falls in the middle of the summer. Fortunately, June, July, and August are typically pleasant. The average high is in the low to mid-60s, and 70s are certainly possible. The warmest reading ever recorded in the park is 91°F (33°C). Another hazard is the utter unpredictability of the weather. "In few mountain locales of the world does the weather change so precipitously and dramatically," wrote Dr. Peter Hackett in the preface to *Surviving Denali.* "A balmy day of glacier travel can rapidly deteriorate into a day of survival-snow-cave digging."[2]

Summertime visitors will have a greater struggle adapting to the sunlight. In late June, the sun rises before 4:30 A.M. and doesn't set until about midnight. As portrayed in the 2002 film *Insomnia,* summer sleep in Alaska can be troubling for the uninitiated.

By September, a hard chill descends upon Denali. Winter arrives in October, in which the average high and low are 31°F (–1°C) and 14°F (–10°C). Usually, more than a foot of snow falls by Halloween. For about six months, the average daytime high is below 32°F (0°C). In January, expect 9°F (–13°C) for a typical high, with a night-time low of –8° F (–22°C)—although temperatures sometimes plummet to –40°F (–40°C), or worse. On one horrific winter night, the temperature

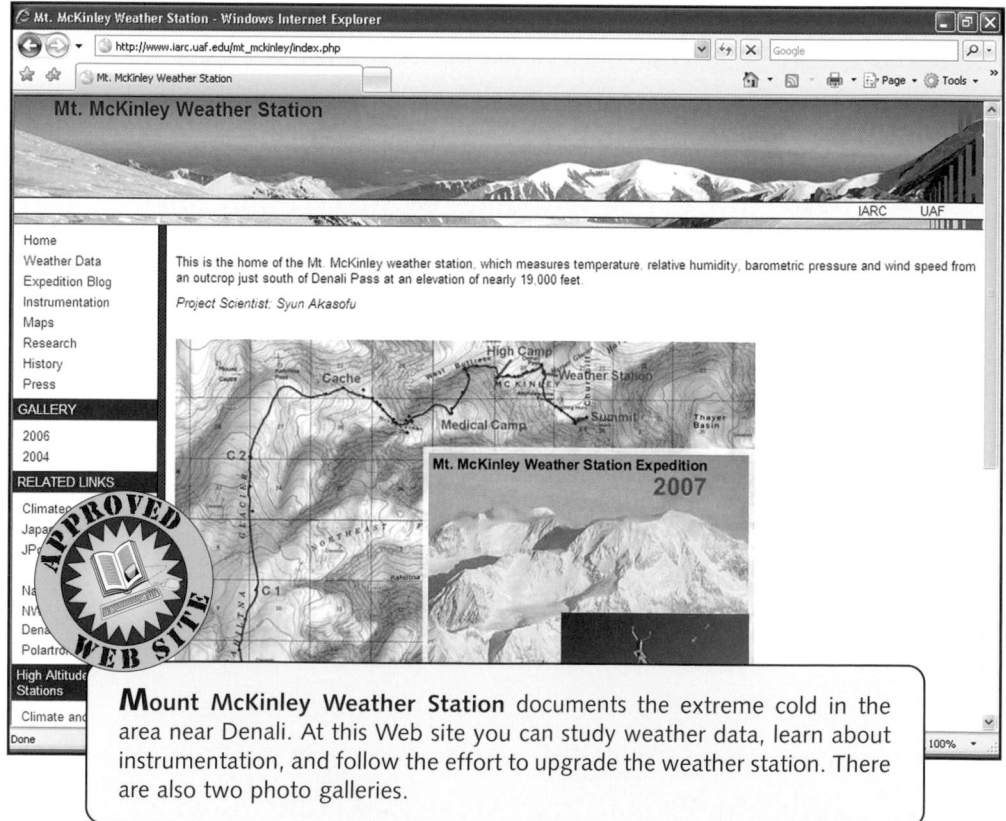

Mount McKinley Weather Station documents the extreme cold in the area near Denali. At this Web site you can study weather data, learn about instrumentation, and follow the effort to upgrade the weather station. There are also two photo galleries.

plunged to −54°F (−48°C). Wrote one resident, "You don't need a thermometer to know when it is cold . . . all you need [to] do is look at the snow: if it's really cold the snow 'sparkles,' like diamonds, in the sunlight."[3]

In the deep forests of Denali, cold is only one of the wintertime evils. Darkness seems almost permanent, with only several hours of light per day. However, the moonlight brightly reflects off the snow, aiding vision. Moreover, the park gets sacked with an average of seven feet (2.13 meters) of snow per year. Animals adapt to the conditions, but life can be harsh for those rangers and other park staffers who remain on their posts in the heart of winter. The cold lingers through April, when highs usually only make it to the 30s. Not until May does spring creep into Denali, with daytime highs climbing into the 50s.

For those thinking about climbing Mt. McKinley, Hackett warns, the weather is inhumanly cold. "Temperatures between the high camp and the summit even in the middle of the summer, are routinely 20° to 40° below and even lower at night," he wrote. "This combination of extreme weather and temperature pummels the unprepared."[4]

➲ HARDY MAMMALS

At Denali, thirty-nine species of mammals have acclimated to the frigid climate. Most of these are "little critters"—squirrels, shrews, muskrats, and beavers. But the park and preserve are also home to the moose, caribou, Dall sheep, wolf, and grizzly bear. At Denali, these fascinating animals are called the "big five."

→ THE MOOSE

When visitors enter the park, the moose is the first animal they are likely to see. And it's hard to miss! The largest deer in the world, the moose stands up to nine feet (2.7 meters) tall and weighs more than 1,200 pounds (544 kilograms). The cow (female) moose has ears like a donkey, but the bull (male) moose grows enormous antlers.

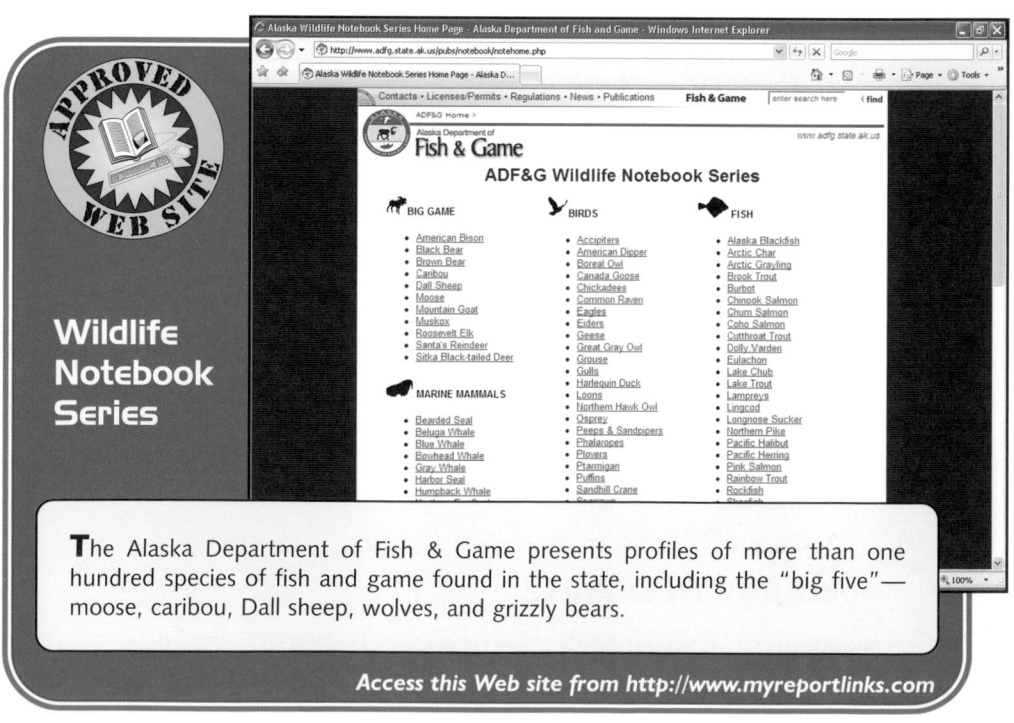

Wildlife Notebook Series

The Alaska Department of Fish & Game presents profiles of more than one hundred species of fish and game found in the state, including the "big five"— moose, caribou, Dall sheep, wolves, and grizzly bears.

Access this Web site from http://www.myreportlinks.com

Moose hang out at lower elevations—often around rivers or in willow patches. As herbivores, they eat grasses as well as the twigs and bark of trees. Amazingly, they can devour up to sixty pounds of such "roughage" in a single day. Although cow moose may appear to be sweet and docile, they are highly protective of their offspring. If they perceive an animal (including a human) as a threat to their young, they will charge after it—and the result isn't pretty.

THE CARIBOU

About eighty years ago, more than twenty thousand caribou roamed Denali NP&P. Now, less than two thousand call Denali home. Like the moose, the caribou is a member of the deer family. But in several ways, the moose and caribou are strikingly different. For one thing, the bull caribou weighs less than four hundred pounds (181 kilograms), and some females tip the scales at less than 200 (91 kilograms). Also, while a bull moose's antlers fan out close to its ears, a caribou's antlers soar several feet above its head. Moreover, the caribou is the only deer in which both the male and female grow antlers.

During the summer months, insects perpetually pester caribou, keeping them constantly on the move. Caribou travel all over the park, although they generally roam above the treelines of the

A Dall sheep ram roaming a hillside in Denali National Park and Preserve.

mountains. Baby calves don't slow the herds down. In fact, a caribou is able to walk just an hour after being born. The next day, it's running around.

THE DALL SHEEP

The Dall sheep may be the prettiest animal in all of Alaska. In addition to its snow-white fur, the Dall sheep has an expressive face with an upturned mouth. It looks like its always smiling. Photographers go on the lookout for baby Dall sheep, which often cuddle underneath their mothers' hindquarters. There is nothing cuter than a Dall sheep lamb popping its head out from underneath its mama and staring sweetly into your eyes.

These sheep are named after William Healey Dall, a naturalist who explored Alaska in the late 1800s. At Denali, they live in high elevations and graze on grasses, flowers, willows, mosses, and lichens. Dall sheep's horns are made up of keratin—the same substance that our fingernails are made of. The female (ewe) Dall sheep has horns, but the male's (ram's) horns are larger. During mating season (November-December), rams butt heads with each other to determine dominance. The crashing of their horns can be heard far away.

THE WOLF

If you happen upon a canine wearing a collar at Denali, do not think it's a lost dog. It very well could be a wolf, some of which wear radio collars as part of a scientific study. These wolves are wild, unpredictable, and powerful enough to kill animals that are much larger than humans.

Wolves feed off such rodents as squirrels and land birds like ptarmigan. They also hunt the large mammals—moose, caribou, and Dall sheep. Other animals thrive because of the wolves. After wolves kill their prey and have their fill of the meat, such animals as wolverines and bears finish the "leftovers."

Wolves usually travel in packs. These typically include a male and female, their offspring, and other nonbreeding adults. The wolves dig dens for their young, and pack members feed the pups regurgitated meat. While on a hunt, wolves sometimes travel thirty miles in a single day. This is not hard for them, since they can run at a top speed of 45 miles per hour (72.4 kilometers per hour). Wolves are also known for their distinctive howl, which punctures the cold air in the evenings and early mornings.

THE GRIZZLY

Grizzly bears are a common sight around Denali—sometimes too common. On Halloween a few years back, people in a residential area spotted a grizzly fighting with a moose, and eventually killing it.

Caribou is another species commonly found in the park. Caribou are also called reindeer.

Although both black bears and grizzlies live at Denali, visitors likely will only see the latter. Black bears live in wooded areas, while grizzlies roam in open areas. So many grizzlies occupy Sable Pass that park officials have closed this area to hiking.

Several hundred grizzlies make Denali their home. They are characterized by the large hump on their shoulders, and they range in color from blond to black. Grizzlies are omnivorous, meaning they eat both meat and vegetation. They feed mostly on berries, grasses, and roots, but they also eat rodents and the calves of moose and caribou. Though the grizzly can weigh more than six hundred pounds (272 kilograms), it is faster than an Olympic sprinter. For short bursts, it can run up to 40 miles per hour (64.4 kilometers per hour).

➲ LITTLE MAMMALS

Along with the "big five," thirty-four other species of mammals live at Denali. Arctic ground squirrels have a dubious distinction: They are the most common mammals in the park, but they are also the most frequently eaten. Animals ranging from bears to golden eagles feast on the furry rodents.

Other mammals include the aggressive and tenacious wolverine as well as the red fox, which is known for its hunting skills. The tiny, adorable pika emits a high-pitched squeak when it feels threatened. The snowshoe hare changes colors each

North American Mammals: Ursus arctos - Windows Internet Explorer

http://www.mnh.si.edu/mna/image_info.cfm?species_id=416

Google

North American Mammals: Ursus arctos

Page · Tools ·

Smithsonian
National Museum of Natural History
North American Mammals

Search the Archive | Carnivora · Ursidae · *Ursus arctos*

· *Species Name*
· *Family Tree*
· *Conservation Status*

Collections

· *Skulls*
· *Bones and Teeth*

Field Guide

· *Map Search*
· *Location Search*
· *About Maps*

Glossary
Teacher Resources
About the Site

Smithsonian Institution

Ursus arctos

Brown Bear, Grizzly Bear

Order: Carnivora
Family: Ursidae

QTVR
Animation
671kb

Conservation Status: The Mexican Grizzly
Bear, *Ursus arcos nelsoni*, is Extinct.

Click to enlarge. (109 kb)

Brown Bears are solitary, powerful predators
who can be aggressive to one another. There is
a social hierarchy: adult males are dominant, and
females with cubs are dominant over juvenile
males and females without cubs. Brown Bears
are omnivorous, consuming everything from
mosses, fungi, herbs, grasses, fruits, berries,
small vertebrates, insects, birds, and
fish—especially salmon during their spawning
run—to other mammals. They dig after
burrowing mammals and take down large

100%

Grizzly bears are common in Denali. On the **Brown Bear, Grizzly Bear** Web page the Smithsonian presents a description of the bear, its activities, and habitat. The page includes photographs, a map, and animation.

season to blend in with its surroundings. In the winter, it is snow white. Hoary marmots are massive rodents who greet each other with a "kiss."

Denali includes many mammals that you aren't likely to find at your local zoo. The list includes the pygmy shrew, little brown bat, coyote, Canada lynx, northern river otter, least weasel, American mink, meadow jumping mouse, North American porcupine, and northern flying squirrel. When the flying squirrel spreads its limbs, its loose skin stretches out like the wings of a hang glider. It can glide through the air up to thirty yards!

The wood frog is the only amphibian living in Denali National Park.

➲167 BIRDS AND A FROG

According to the National Park Service, 167 species of birds have been recorded in Denali. The great majority are migratory, coming from six different continents. These birds arrive in the spring and high-tail it out of there when the autumn chill settles in.

Arctic terns are among the frequent flyers. They travel from Antarctica to the northern climbs every year—a twenty-thousand-mile (32,187-kilometer) round-trip. The bald eagle, the symbol of America, doesn't leave the continent. Alaskans proudly boast that their state has more bald eagles than all the other states combined. At Denali, the golden eagle is even more common. The gyrfalcon also makes its presence felt at the park. The largest falcon in the world [four-foot (1.2-meter) wingspan], this bird is extremely fast and powerful. It attacks, kills, and eats squirrels and other ground animals.

Some species live at Denali year-round, including the black-capped chickadees, which have been called "barracudas with wings."[5] Though weighing only a half-ounce, these teeny songbirds survive the winter and seize prey with powerful bills. The common redpoll can endure extremely cold temperatures. All three kinds of ptarmigan—rock, willow, and white-tailed—make Denali their full-time home. Thick feathers on their feet allow them to walk on frozen ground. The willow

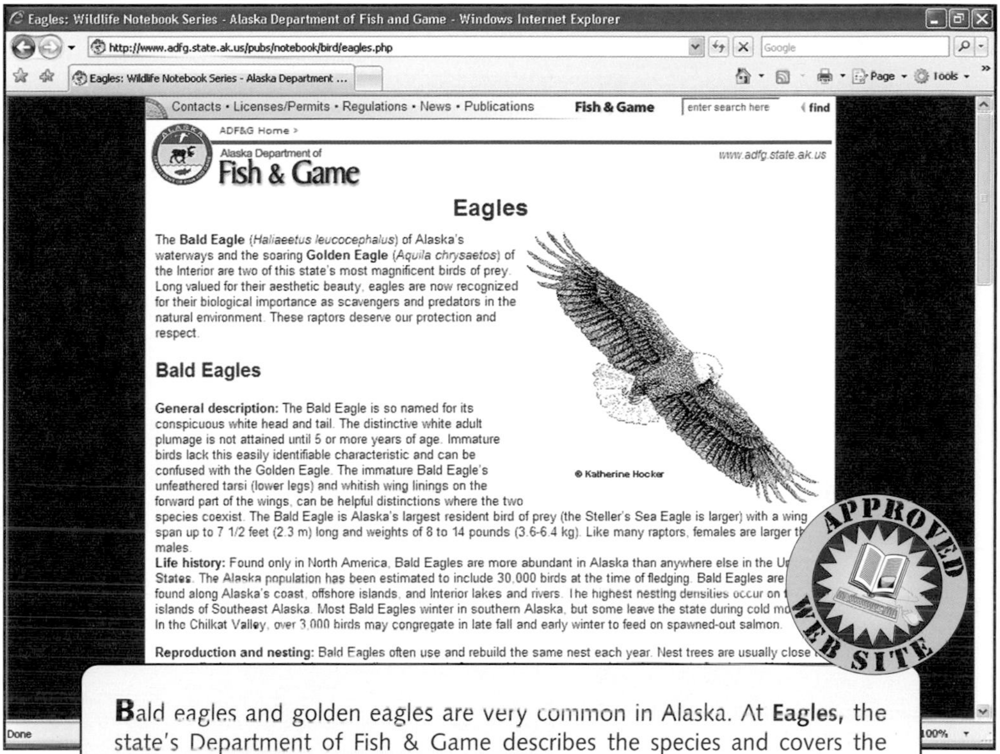

Eagles: Wildlife Notebook Series - Alaska Department of Fish and Game - Windows Internet Explorer

http://www.adfg.state.ak.us/pubs/notebook/bird/eagles.php

Eagles: Wildlife Notebook Series - Alaska Department ...

Contacts • Licenses/Permits • Regulations • News • Publications **Fish & Game** enter search here ‹ find

ADF&G Home >

Alaska Department of
Fish & Game

www.adfg.state.ak.us

Eagles

The **Bald Eagle** (*Haliaeetus leucocephalus*) of Alaska's
waterways and the soaring **Golden Eagle** (*Aquila chrysaetos*) of
the Interior are two of this state's most magnificent birds of prey.
Long valued for their aesthetic beauty, eagles are now recognized
for their biological importance as scavengers and predators in the
natural environment. These raptors deserve our protection and
respect.

Bald Eagles

General description: The Bald Eagle is so named for its
conspicuous white head and tail. The distinctive white adult
plumage is not attained until 5 or more years of age. Immature
birds lack this easily identifiable characteristic and can be
confused with the Golden Eagle. The immature Bald Eagle's
unfeathered tarsi (lower legs) and whitish wing linings on the
forward part of the wings, can be helpful distinctions where the two
species coexist. The Bald Eagle is Alaska's largest resident bird of prey (the Steller's Sea Eagle is larger) with a wing
span up to 7 1/2 feet (2.3 m) long and weights of 8 to 14 pounds (3.6-6.4 kg). Like many raptors, females are larger than
males.
Life history: Found only in North America, Bald Eagles are more abundant in Alaska than anywhere else in the United
States. The Alaska population has been estimated to include 30,000 birds at the time of fledging. Bald Eagles are
found along Alaska's coast, offshore islands, and Interior lakes and rivers. The highest nesting densities occur on the
islands of Southeast Alaska. Most Bald Eagles winter in southern Alaska, but some leave the state during cold months.
In the Chilkat Valley, over 3,000 birds may congregate in late fall and early winter to feed on spawned-out salmon.

Reproduction and nesting: Bald Eagles often use and rebuild the same nest each year. Nest trees are usually close

© Katherine Hocker

Bald eagles and golden eagles are very common in Alaska. At **Eagles,** the state's Department of Fish & Game describes the species and covers the birds' life history, reproduction, nesting, diet, management, and protection.

ptarmigan couldn't leave the state if it wanted to:
It is Alaska's state bird.

Finally, we come to Denali's amphibians—or
amphibian. Of the six thousand varieties in the
world, only one lives in this vast territory: the
wood frog. Though only several centimeters long,
this is one tough frog. Like some other animals, it
possesses "cryoprotectant" chemicals that allow it
to survive freezing temperatures. Throughout the
winter, the wood frog remains inanimate and, in
fact, freezes solid. In spring, it thaws out and hops
on its merry way.

A visitor drives through Denali National Park. Because of its remote location, officials at Denali do not have to deal with as much pollution as parks that get more traffic.

Big Issues

Look outside your window. How far can you see? If you lived in Anchorage and it was a sunny day, you could see Mt. McKinley—more than 130 miles (209 kilometers) away.

Alaska's air is cleaner than that of any other state. Moreover, Denali's air is especially pure. Notes the National Park Service: "Denali is the only Class I air quality area of significant size in Alaska, which under the Clean Air Act was set aside to receive the most stringent degree of air quality protection."[1]

Human visitors, even those with the best intentions, could wreak havoc on a national park. Pollution from automobiles (or nearby factories) could contaminate the air. Microorganisms on the bottom of a boat could get into a park's lakes and kill its fish, and those animals that prey on fish could subsequently die. Such chain reactions could affect many of the fish, birds, mammals, and vegetation of an ecosystem. National parks were created to preserve the land, not destroy it. Thus, at each national park, scientists work hard to maintain the ecosystem.

Such is the case at Denali NP&P. Its "protectors" fortunately do not have to deal with many major environmental issues—like they do at, for example, Yellowstone National Park. Denali's subarctic climate, its grand size, and relatively few tourists per acre prevent harm to the ecosystem. Nevertheless, park officials and scientists monitor the park's natural environment. They study the climate, glaciers, geologic processes, fire ecology, and pollution. Below are some of the big issues swirling around Denali. They include not just environmental concerns but mountain climbing, wildfires, earthquakes, grizzly bears, and even dinosaurs!

→ EXOTIC PLANTS

They may look lovely on a windowsill, but no rangers want them in their national park. Exotic plants are defined as those that grow in a given place only as the result of human action. Such plants can destroy other plants, which can eliminate food sources for certain animals. One herb, bird vetch, is the scourge of many national parks. It invades stands of native tree saplings and shrubs, and it climbs and spreads over native plants.

Compared to most other national parks, exotic plant species have not been as big of a problem in Alaska's national parks, including Denali. One reason is that few exotic plants are able to grow in Alaska's frigid soil. Nevertheless, with 400,000

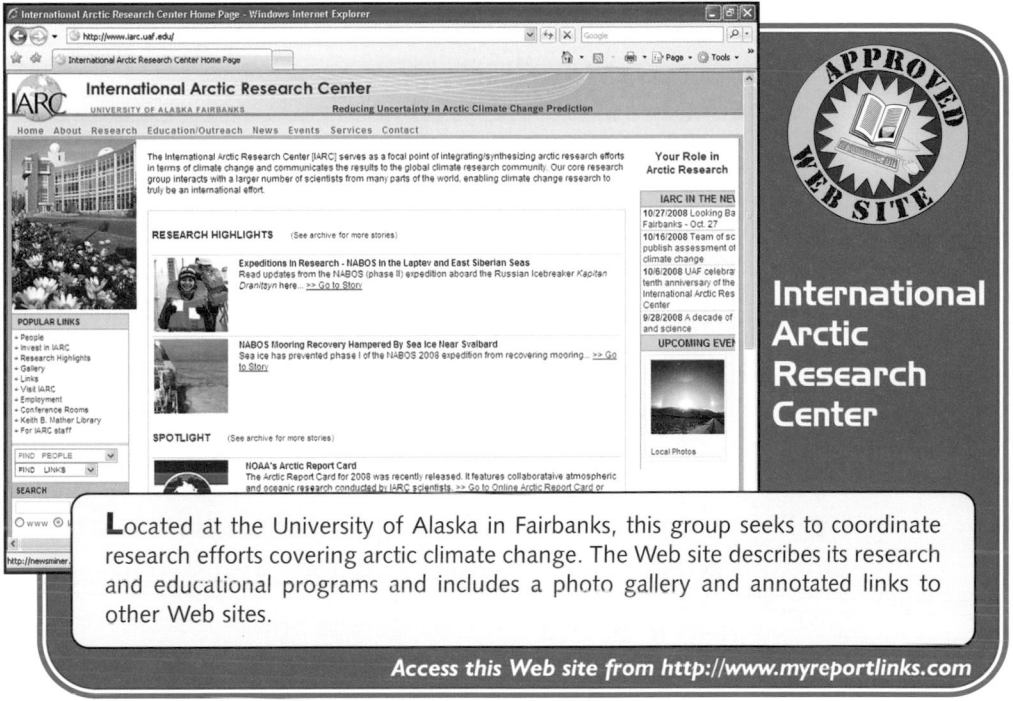

Located at the University of Alaska in Fairbanks, this group seeks to coordinate research efforts covering arctic climate change. The Web site describes its research and educational programs and includes a photo gallery and annotated links to other Web sites.

Access this Web site from http://www.myreportlinks.com

visitors trekking through Denali every year, it has become a bigger issue. In addition, climate change has made the park warmer, allowing some invasive species to thrive. New exotic plants are appearing, and some existing exotics are spreading. Fortunately, these foreign plants are limited to areas near the park road. Park officials will need to work hard to keep it that way.

MANAGING FIRE

Decades ago, if a fire erupted in a national park, firefighters would sometimes arrive to "limit the damage." Over time, scientists realized that fire is a natural part of a region's ecosystem. After fires wipe out sections of forest, new vegetation eventually rises from the ashes.

Fires have scorched Denali's land for thousands of years. The park's northwest area is particularly vulnerable due to dry conditions and an abundance of black spruce. At Denali, officials are concerned not for the trees but for the park's structures—cabins, homes, offices, and visitor centers. Over the last several years, workers have removed trees and other vegetation from around many of these buildings. They hope that wildfires will end at these buffer zones and leave the structures untouched. Ideally, this would allow rescue workers to swoop down via helicopter and save the buildings' inhabitants.

HUNDREDS OF EARTHQUAKES

If you were to look at satellite photos of the Alaska Range, you would think that a canal had been dug through it. The "canal" is actually the gigantic Denali Fault, which runs through the mountain range from east to west. A fault is a crack in the earth's crust, and its existence leads to earthquakes.

Denali experiences approximately six hundred seismic events each year. Virtually all of these earthquakes are so small that people do not even know they are occurring. But once in a great while, an especially large quake will shake up the

National Parks Conservation Association | Protecting Our National Parks for Future Generations - Windows Internet Explorer

http://www.npca.org/

National Parks Conservation Association | Protecting ...

National Parks Conservation Association®
Protecting Our National Parks for Future Generations®

search   GO

How You Can Help
→ Donate Now
→ Join Online
→ Renew Membership
→ Planned Giving
→ Take Action

FIND A NPCA REGIONAL OFFICE OR CENTER:
Select One   Map

INFORMATION FOR:
Select One

Bear in Katmai National Park & Preserve, Alaska
© David Tipling/Digital Vision/Getty Images

| Who We Are | What We Do | Where We Work | Explore the Parks | Donate Now | Take Action | News and Publications |

IN THE SPOTLIGHT

Our National Parks

NPCA's new public service ads point out that chronic federal funding shortfalls have put national parks at risk. Sign our petition and encourage the incoming Administration and Congress to protect our national parks for our children and grandchildren.
Sign Our Petition Today >>
See the Advertisements >>

Action Items

SIGN UP FOR NEWS + ALERTS

enter email   GO

→ **Tell the next Administration and Congress to protect our national parks**

→ **Support funding for the Land and Water Conservation Fund**

TAKE ACTION >

NATIONAL PARKS MAGAZINE

National PARKS

National Parks, our award-winning quarterly magazine, exclusively of members of NPCA.
Read More

SUBSCRIBE

APPROVED WEB SITE

The **National Parks Conservation Association** runs education and advocacy programs to help protect the parks for future generations. Its Web site summarizes the group's involvement in park issues and covers wildlife protection, park history, and marine life.

Done   100%

staff and tourists. On May 21, 1991, a massive earthquake rocked Mt. McKinley, with mountain climbers reporting multiple avalanches. Two earthquakes in the fall of 2000 rattled local residents. As mentioned in Chapter 3, a record-breaking quake on November 3, 2002, knocked items off shelves and damaged roads.

Alaskans take earthquakes seriously. The state experiences more than 20,000 seismic events a year, and a quake killed more than 130 state residents in 1964. At Denali, officials work with the Alaska Earthquake Information Center (and other groups) to monitor and study seismic activity around the park. The more Alaskans understand earthquakes, the more prepared they can be.

⊜DEATHS ON MT. McKINLEY

For more than a hundred years, people have tried to climb to the top of Mt. McKinley. Park officials have long worried about the dangers of ascending the High One, but never have they made the mountain off-limits. After 1992, when thirteen people died on Mt. McKinley and Mt. Foraker, the park enforced new safety measures.

Today, climbers have to register and pay $200 in fees in order to take on Mt. McKinley. Park officials provide climbers with educational materials tailored to the person's level of experience. Moreover, climbers are strongly urged to ascend the mountain with an experienced guide.

Despite these safety precautions, park officials can do nothing to prevent extreme weather and fatal falls. Though no one died on Mt. McKinley in 2006, five people lost their lives before June in 2007.

On May 18, 2007, the bodies of Andre Callari and Brian Postlethwait, both of Utah, were discovered. They had been killed by an avalanche. Just days earlier, Mizuki Takahashi and partner Brian Massey fell 2,000 feet (610 meters) to their deaths. Another climber, Lara-Karena Kellogg of

NOVA | Deadly Ascent | PBS - Windows Internet Explorer

http://www.pbs.org/wgbh/nova/denali/

Google

NOVA | Deadly Ascent | PBS

Page · Tools

PBS HOME   PROGRAMS A-Z   TV SCHEDULES   SUPPORT PBS   SHOP PBS   SEARCH PBS

NOVA SCIENCE PROGRAMMING ON AIR AND ONLINE

SEARCH NOVA

NOVA HOME   TV SCHEDULE   ARCHIVE   ABOUT NOVA   SUBSCRIBE   TEACHERS   RSS   FEEDBACK   TRANSCRIPTS   SHOP NOVA   WATCH NOVA ONLINE   FAQs

A team of doctors and climbers on Denali test the body's response to extreme cold.

Corporate funding provided by

DEADLY ASCENT

ARTICLE & DISPATCHES

Predicting Survival
Can medical science forecast why some people get sick climbing at high altitude while others don't?

Dispatches
Read accounts of the Spring 2000 expedition sent in from the field.

INTERACTIVES

Climb Denali
Explore the demanding route from base camp to the 20,320-foot summit.

Survival Skills
What are the basic skills anyone heading into the mountains should have?

Body Breakdowns
See how extreme cold can

RESOURCES

TV Program Description
Airing on PBS Tuesday December 2 at 8 pm
Check local listings as dates and times may vary.

Links & Books

Denali For Kids
In this kids-eye view of Mt. McKinley, find out what the NOVA team ate for dinner, see what high altitude can do to your body, and more.

Teacher's Guide

more energy.
fewer emissions.

APPROVED WEB SITE

Deadly **Ascent** is the companion site to a PBS TV program showcasing efforts to climb Denali. The focus is on survival and effects on climbers' bodies, such as mountain sickness.

EDITOR'S CHOICE

Seattle, lost her life while rappelling down part of Mt. Wake.

Every time a climber dies on Mt. McKinley, controversy arises. In one online forum after the deaths of Callari and Postlethwait, one person wrote: "Is it worth losing a life for one moment of glory?"[2] But a proponent of mountain climbing responded: "Do you want to live your entire life in your safe little bubble?"[3] Unless or until they're faced with large death tolls, park officials will continue to let people summit Mt. McKinley—or die trying.

→LAND OF DINOSAURS

On June 27, 2005, Dr. Paul McCarthy led his University of Alaska Fairbanks geology students on an exploration of Denali NP&P. At Igloo Creek near the park road, he explained that the Cretaceous sedimentary rock that they were examining was the type that preserved dinosaur tracks (footprints). Student Susi Tomsich spotted such a track and said, "Like this one?"[4]

Yes, like that one! Tomsich didn't realize it, but she became the first person to discover dinosaur tracks in Denali. Scientists estimated that the fossil was 65 million to 70 million years old. As for the type of dinosaur, it likely was a three-toed

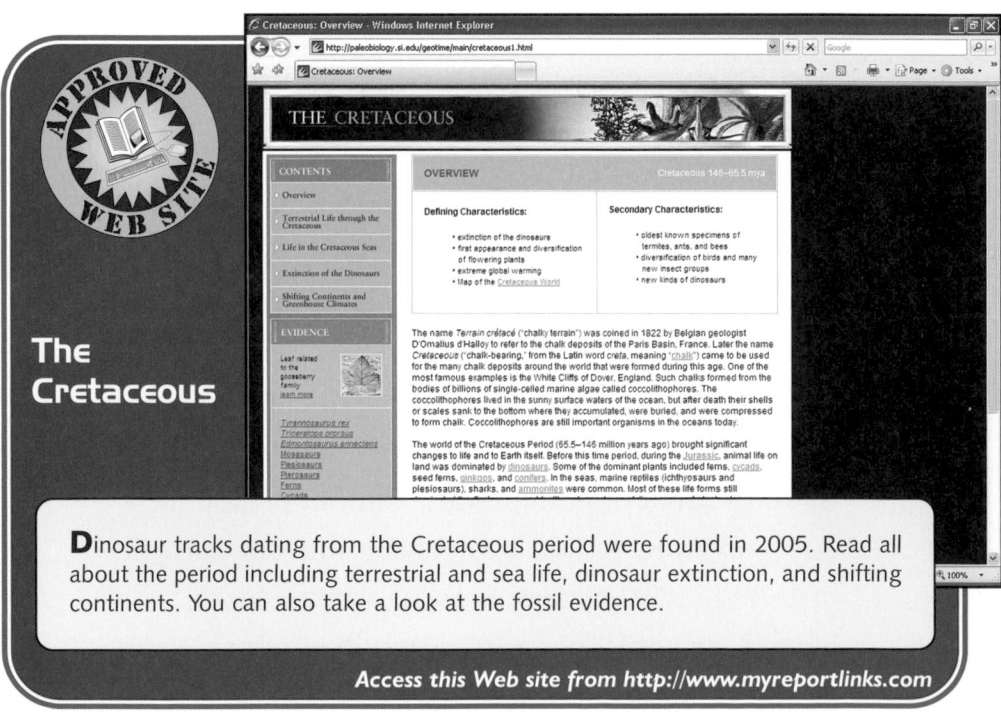

The Cretaceous

Dinosaur tracks dating from the Cretaceous period were found in 2005. Read all about the period including terrestrial and sea life, dinosaur extinction, and shifting continents. You can also take a look at the fossil evidence.

Access this Web site from http://www.myreportlinks.com

theropod (a meat-eater that walked on its hind legs). Its nine-inch (22.9-centimeter) foot indicated that it stood approximately ten feet (three meters) tall and weighed between one hundred and two hundred pounds (45.4 to 90.7 kilograms).

Tomsich's discovery generated tremendous excitement and a great deal of paleontological activity in Denali. The following summer, many more trace fossil sites were located in the Igloo Canyon and Double Mountain vicinities of the park. Scientists discovered mostly theropod tracks, but they also found footprints of several hadrosaurs (duck-billed dinosaurs). More research will continue in Denali, which dinosaur researcher Tony Fiorillo referred to as the "great paleontological candy store."[5]

PROTECTING THE WILDLIFE

As in all national parks, rangers at Denali tell visitors not to disturb the wildlife. They hammer home this message through presentations, literature, and whatever other way possible. The No. 1 rule is, of course, *don't feed the animals.* Doing so alters their diet and makes them come back for more—which puts both people and the animals at risk.

Rangers allow visitors to observe animals from a distance. However, people should never follow or approach animals. Doing so disrupts their natural

In most instances, a bear sighting is a harmless encounter. However, it is important for park visitors not to feed the bears or leave food out for them.

patterns of behavior and puts the person at risk. Though rare, animals at national parks do attack people—and sometimes kill them. Animals are particularly dangerous when they're caring for their young as well as during mating season. At Denali, bears are of particular concern.

➲ BE AWARE OF THE BEARS

One day, author/photographer Aubrey Stephen Johnson explored Denali with his wife, Marilyn. Suddenly, Aubrey heard Marilyn emit "two piercing screams." He recalled: "Marilyn was crouched against the edge of a steep, upward sloping bank, arms covering her head, her back toward a huge honey-colored grizzly approaching at a rolling run." Revealed Marilyn: "I knew that any second I would feel the claws in my back. I was in complete panic. . . ."[6] Fortunately, the bear ran away.

Bear maulings are rare at Denali, but grizzlies and black bears are an ever-present concern. The park provides literature on bear safety. Rules and guidelines include:

• Keep your camp clean. Bears are attracted to whatever is edible. Food and even toiletries need to be stored in a closed vehicle or food locker. Garbage must be tossed into bear-proof garbage cans. These are not recommendations but park requirements.

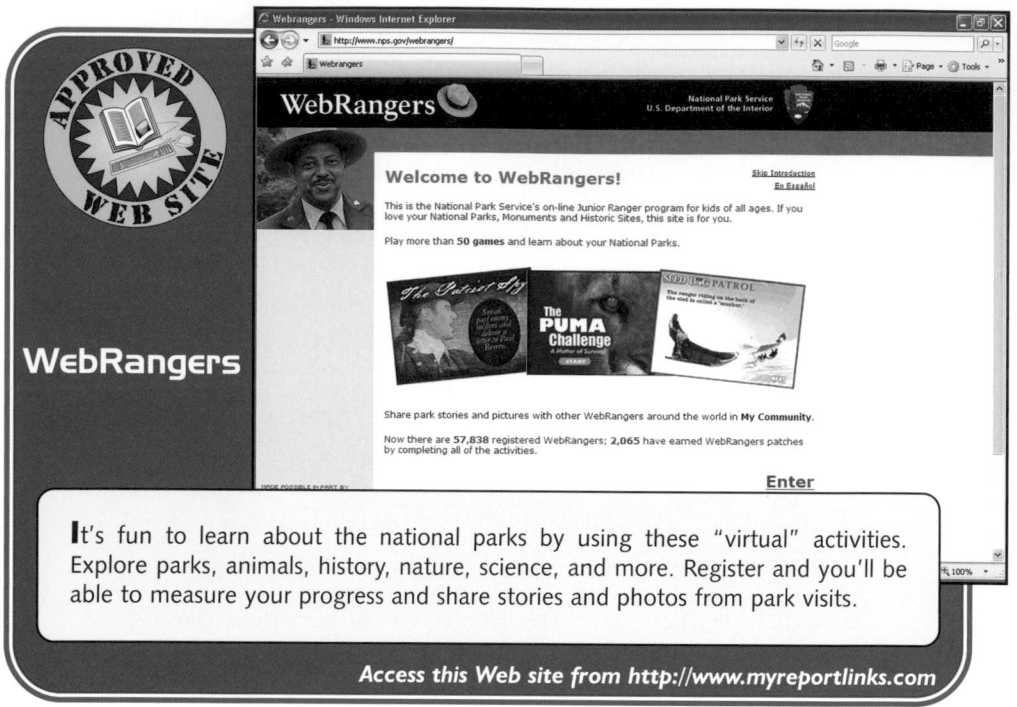

WebRangers

It's fun to learn about the national parks by using these "virtual" activities. Explore parks, animals, history, nature, science, and more. Register and you'll be able to measure your progress and share stories and photos from park visits.

Access this Web site from http://www.myreportlinks.com

• Keep your distance from a bear. It is illegal to approach within a quarter-mile of this animal.

• Hike in groups of three or more. Bears are scared off by groups of people and all the noise they make.

• Similarly, don't hike alone. It's your greatest chance of encountering a bear.

• If you sense that a bear is in your general vicinity, speak in a loud voice, which would likely scare it off. However, do not startle a bear.

• Stay away from a bear's cubs and food. Otherwise, an adult bear will consider you a threat.

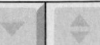

• If you have a close encounter with a bear, stay calm and slowly back away. Do not run or scream, for such behavior could provoke a bear to chase you. Forget about climbing a tree, for bears can climb much better than people.

Now that you have learned the do's and don'ts of Denali, it is time to enjoy your visit!

Chapter 6

One of the most common ways to explore Denali National Park is by foot. This pedestrian bridge allows visitors to cross the Savage River.

Exploring Denali

Traveling to Denali National Park & Preserve is no ordinary vacation. For virtually everyone, it is far, far away. The journey there is usually long and tedious—and probably expensive. The cold weather (even in the summer) and endless daylight can be disturbing. Many have squawked about the bumpy bus ride along the park's lone (unpaved) road. Others have complained that they couldn't see Mt. McKinley or enough wild animals. Still others have lost their lives in this unforgiving wilderness—many while climbing mountains and others by succumbing to killer storms.

Yet done right, a Denali vacation can be an exhilarating, even life-changing experience. The eight national parks of Alaska are more pristine—less tainted by civilization—than those of the continental United States. They are also enormous, encompassing two-thirds of all national park land. But of the eight, Denali is the most accessible. Thus, it offers visitors the best opportunity to experience the great Alaskan wilderness.

→GETTING THERE

Denali is close to Alaska's two largest cities. How-ever, in this expansive state, "close" is a relative term. Anchorage is 237 miles (381 kilometers) from the park's entrance, and Fairbanks is 120 miles (193 kilometers) away. The paved George Parks Highway leads from both cities to Denali.

Many vacationers fly to the Fairbanks Inter-national Airport or the Ted Stevens Anchorage International Airport. From there, they can either drive to Denali in a rental vehicle or take a bus or train. The Alaska Railroad offers deluxe travel accommodations and magnificent views. Some wealthy travelers fly from Anchorage to Denali via Talkeetna Aero Services—at close to $500 per ticket.

Besides making transportation reservations, travelers must book ahead for lodging or camp-sites. If you're planning a July visit, you'll want to make reservations before March. Also, be careful about the dates you choose. The tourist season runs from mid-May to mid-September, and the only "safe" months to visit (in terms of weather) are June, July, and August.

Though it is expensive to get to Denali, it is cheap to get into the park. A seven-day pass costs just $10 per person or $20 per vehicle. Yet you

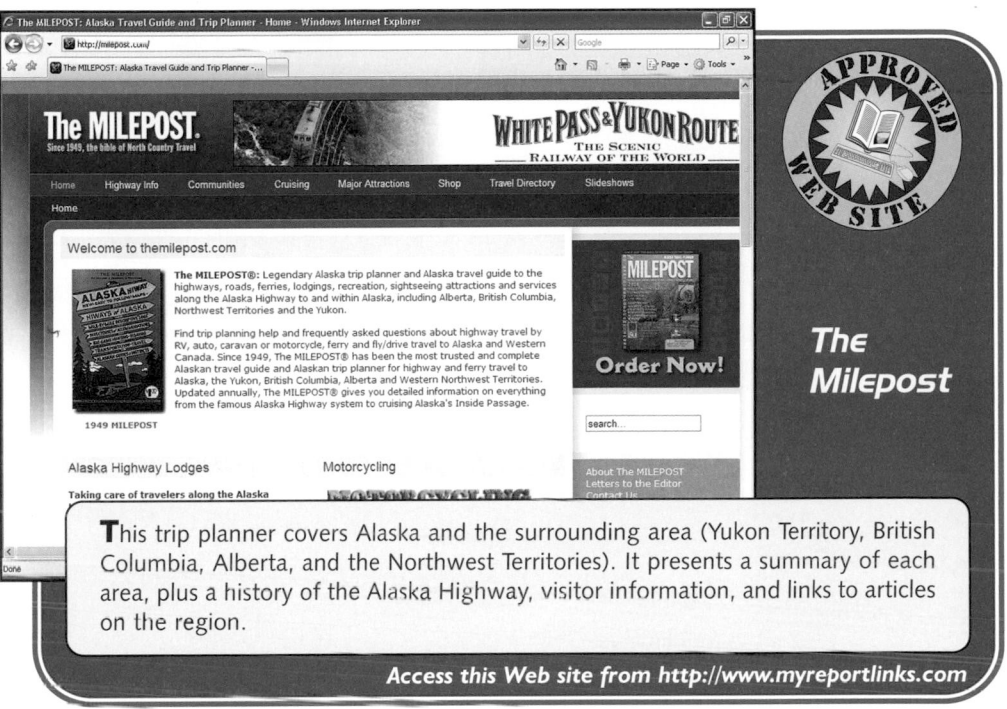

This trip planner covers Alaska and the surrounding area (Yukon Territory, British Columbia, Alberta, and the Northwest Territories). It presents a summary of each area, plus a history of the Alaska Highway, visitor information, and links to articles on the region.

Access this Web site from http://www.myreportlinks.com

cannot drive through Denali. Vehicles are permitted only for the first few miles of the park road. Unless you're a rugged adventurer, the only way to explore Denali is by bus. Here, too, you will need to make reservations in advance.

→ THE BUS TRIP

Most visitors explore the park via the green shuttle buses. You can buy four different round-trip tickets. One takes you fifty-three miles (85.3 kilometers) down the road to the Toklat River, while another journeys sixty-three miles (101.4 kilometers) to Fish Creek Turnaround. Wonder Lake is eighty-five miles (136.8 kilometers) away,

The ever-present green buses are the most common way for campers and other tourists to travel through the park.

while the journey to Kantishna (the end of the road) is ninety-five miles. If you're afraid of heights, you might want to choose the short Toklat River trip. Past that point, the road climbs to great heights without guardrails.

Because the buses stop frequently for sightseeing, the round-trip journeys take between five and twelve hours. Tickets range from $19 to $36 for adults, but they're free for kids ages fourteen and under. One piece of advice: limit your liquid intake. The shuttle buses have no restrooms, and bathroom breaks are only once every hour and a half.

Denali has a whole fleet of buses. Camper buses take visitors to their campgrounds, while the Riley Creek Loop shuttles visitors from one facility to another. Many tourists buy tickets for deluxe tour buses, which are more comfortable than the school bus-type shuttles. The Denali Natural History Tour bus stops for a presentation by an Alaskan Native, which may include singing or storytelling.

⊜ SUCH SIGHTS TO SEE

Shuttle and tour buses take you deep into the wilderness. Through your window, you'll witness the full splendor of Denali: taiga forest, wildflowers, large rivers that flow down the Alaska Range— even colorful volcanic cliffs. Special highlights include:

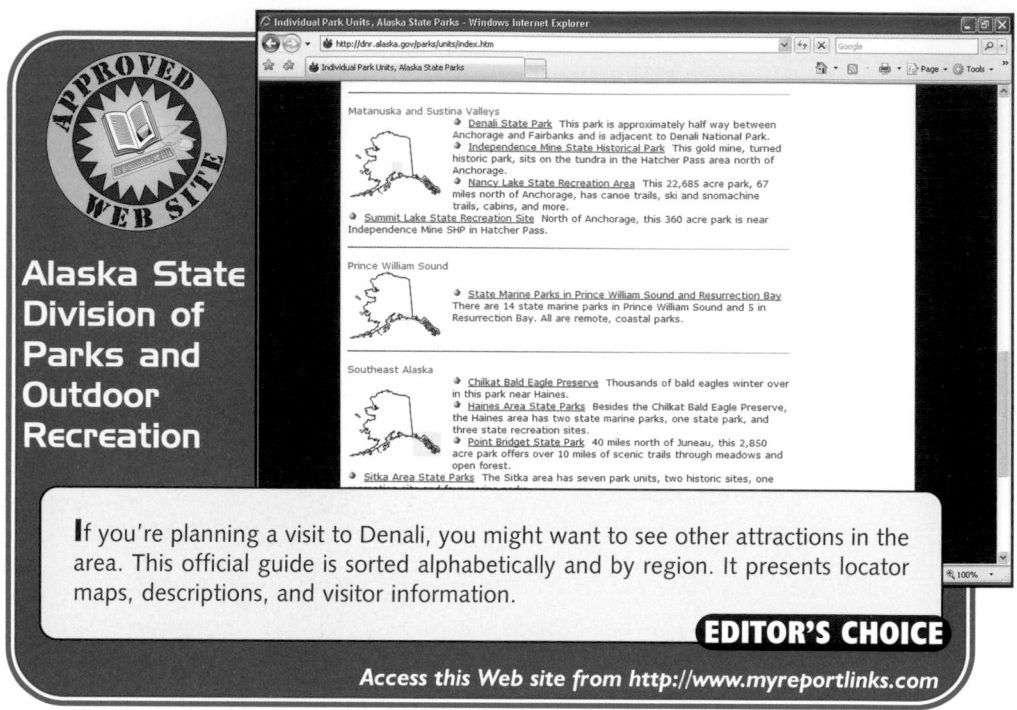

Alaska State Division of Parks and Outdoor Recreation

Individual Park Units, Alaska State Parks - Windows Internet Explorer

http://dnr.alaska.gov/parks/units/index.htm

Individual Park Units, Alaska State Parks

Matanuska and Sustina Valleys
- Denali State Park This park is approximately half way between Anchorage and Fairbanks and is adjacent to Denali National Park.
- Independence Mine State Historical Park This gold mine, turned historic park, sits on the tundra in the Hatcher Pass area north of Anchorage.
- Nancy Lake State Recreation Area This 22,685 acre park, 67 miles north of Anchorage, has canoe trails, ski and snomachine trails, cabins, and more.
- Summit Lake State Recreation Site North of Anchorage, this 360 acre park is near Independence Mine SHP in Hatcher Pass.

Prince William Sound
- State Marine Parks in Prince William Sound and Resurrection Bay There are 14 state marine parks in Prince William Sound and 5 in Resurrection Bay. All are remote, coastal parks.

Southeast Alaska
- Chilkat Bald Eagle Preserve Thousands of bald eagles winter over in this park near Haines.
- Haines Area State Parks Besides the Chilkat Bald Eagle Preserve, the Haines area has two state marine parks, one state park, and three state recreation sites.
- Point Bridget State Park 40 miles north of Juneau, this 2,850 acre park offers over 10 miles of scenic trails through meadows and open forest.
- Sitka Area State Parks The Sitka area has seven park units, two historic sites, one

If you're planning a visit to Denali, you might want to see other attractions in the area. This official guide is sorted alphabetically and by region. It presents locator maps, descriptions, and visitor information.

EDITOR'S CHOICE

Access this Web site from http://www.myreportlinks.com

Mile 29: Teklanika River. This is one of Denali's many braided rivers, in which streams wander down enormous gravel streambeds.

Mile 34: Craggy Igloo Mountain. Bring your binoculars, because far off in these mountains Dall sheep tend to roam.

Miles 38–43: Sable Pass. Here is where you begin to clutch your seat, as the road wends higher and higher. Bears search for food on Sable Pass, especially during the fall.

Mile 46: Polychrome Pass. The views here are spectacular, especially of the mountains' multicolored rock. Caribou can be seen in the valleys below.

Mile 53: Toklat River. Bears, caribou, and wolves gather in this braided river. This is also the turnaround point for those on the short shuttle tour. Outhouses are provided, but plumbing does not exist this deep into the park.

Mile 58: Highway Pass. This is the highest point on the road and the first chance to see Mt. McKinley, some forty miles (64.4 kilometers) away. Hope for a clear day, since clouds usually shroud the mighty mountain.

Mile 64: Thorofare Pass. Look around for bears and caribou — if you can keep your eyes open. On this narrow and twisting road, a tour bus went off the road and crashed in 1981, killing five passengers

▲ The beautiful and peaceful Wonder Lake is one of the most popular spots in Denali National Park and Preserve.

and injuring twenty-five others. Buses have made thousands of successful trips since, but the incident reminds us that safety is not guaranteed at Denali.

Mile 66: Eielson Visitor Center. Park rangers are available to guide you on tundra walks or for other assistance. This area is one of the best places to see Mt. McKinley.

Mile 68: Muldrow Glacier. Climbers used to climb this famous hunk of ice to reach the summit of Mt. McKinley.

Mile 86: Wonder Lake. In 1947 the legendary Ansel Adams photographed Mt. McKinley towering over this peaceful body of water. People continue to purchase this spectacular image as artwork for

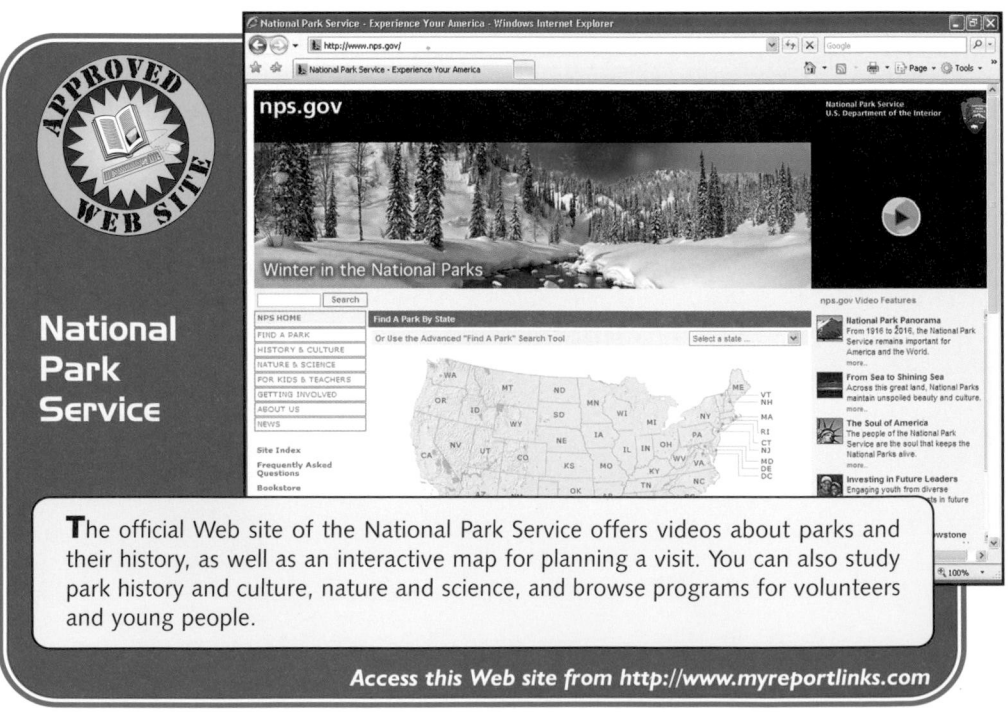

National Park Service

The official Web site of the National Park Service offers videos about parks and their history, as well as an interactive map for planning a visit. You can also study park history and culture, nature and science, and browse programs for volunteers and young people.

Access this Web site from http://www.myreportlinks.com

their walls. At Wonder Lake, the High One is only twenty-seven miles (43.5 kilometers) away.

Mile 95: Kantishna. Talk about your remote towns! Located at the end of the road, Kantishna boasts a summer population of approximately 135 and a winter population of zero. In 1905 thousands of miners flocked to Kantishna Hills, but they all left when the gold ran out.

For the best chance of spotting animals on your bus tour, begin your trip at the crack of dawn. Animals are more active in the early morning hours. Reports "BudgetQueen" in Fodor's *Alaska 2007:* "I am always on the first bus out—just my preference. I also make the drive to Savage River while there, and have always seen something. Last trip I watched three bears for close to an hour on the wash-out before Savage River. Binoculars are necessary."[1]

NECESSITIES

As long as you don't venture off into the backcountry, you should feel safe and secure in Denali. The Canyon Health Clinic Urgent Care Center is located near the park entrance, and the Alaska State Troopers operate a post in nearby Healy. You can always call 911, although cell phones don't work when you stray too far from the main road. The Denali General Store and the Riley Creek Mercantile sell groceries, camping supplies, and other necessities.

These backpackers are crossing the rocky terrain of the mountainous region in Denali National Park.

⇒ CAMPING

Most of Denali's overnight visitors sleep with a roof over their heads. But some hardy souls prefer the great outdoors—even though summer night-time temperatures can drop into the 20s.

Denali offers eight campgrounds with a total of about three hundred sites. These grounds include Riley Creek, Marino, Savage River, Savage Group, Sanctuary River, Teklanika River, Igloo Creek, and Wonder Lake. All are just off the main road. Each campground takes reservations (which are highly recommended), and most are open from May to September. The camping fees are cheap: $12 for those with flush toilets, and $6 for pit-toilet grounds. All of the campgrounds provide running water.

The Riley Creek Campground, located next to the park's entrance, is the only one that's open year-round. It is the largest of the campgrounds (one hundred sites), and it is one of three camp-grounds that allow RVs. With the exception of remote Wonder Lake, all of the campgrounds are within thirty-four miles of the park's entrance. For the Sanctuary River, Igloo River, and Wonder Lake campgrounds, you must take a camper bus to your destination.

Fires are permitted at the campgrounds, but only on established fire grates. The park provides a list of camping rules, some of which are detailed in Chapter 5.

Visitors can camp in the backcountry, but they need to acquire a permit to do so. They also will receive a long list of dos and don'ts. Officials advise campers not to drink river water unless they boil it or use a specific filter. Giardia, a waterborne cyst, exists in the park, and it can cause severe intestinal illness.

Several commercial campgrounds exist within a few miles of the park. These are more expensive, but they offer more conveniences. At the Denali Grizzly Bear Cabins and Campground, you can rent a cabin with a bathroom and a stove for $248 a night.

⊜ LODGING

Yes, lodging exists within Denali Park. You can stay only in Kantishna, at the end of the park road, and some of the accommodations are primitive. At Kantishna's Camp Denali cabins, only outhouses and shared bathhouses are provided. The Kantishna Roadhouse is for those who want to "rough it" in style. It features an attractive lobby and such amenities as a restaurant and sauna. But the rooms are $360 a night. The Caribou Lodge is so remote that you can only get there by small plane. Hosts Pam and Mike Nickols lead their guests on hikes and canoe trips. They even teach them how to drive a team of sled dogs over the snow.

Most tourists stay in accommodations just outside the park. The Denali Princess Lodge and the

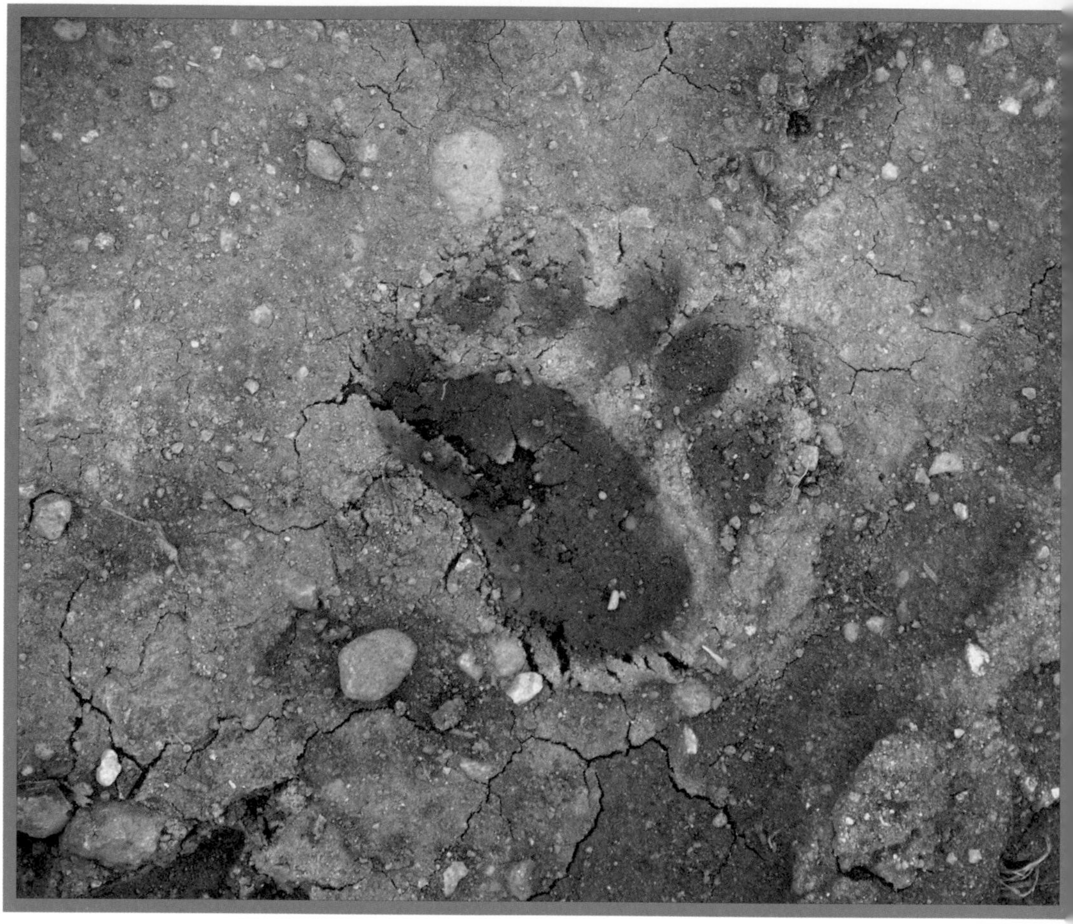

▲ *When you are hiking through Denali's wilderness you may come across a bear print such as this one.*

McKinley Chalet Resort both sit just one mile from the park entrance. In addition to magnificent views of the Denali wilderness, they offer comfortable rooms with phones and televisions. However, each of these hotels (and others) is owned by the Princess and Holland American cruise lines. Most of the rooms go to cruise passengers.

Tourists have an easier time reserving rooms at three lodgings near the park: Denali Bluffs Hotel,

Grande Denali Lodge, and Denali Crow's Nest Log Cabins. All three are located on mountainsides overlooking the Nenana Canyon. Rooms are simple and rates are high, but the views are breathtaking.

Other visitors stay in Healy, a coal town ten miles north of the entrance. At Healy's bed & breakfasts, the hosts try their best to make you feel at home. At the Earthsong Lodge restaurant, they will pack a sack lunch for you to take to the park. Other vacationers stay a few miles south of Denali. At the Cedar Hotel at Denali Grizzly Bear Resort, you can hear the rushing water of the nearby Nenana River.

HIKING IN THE WILDERNESS

Unlike most national parks, very few hiking trails exist at Denali. You are free to hike, but the experience is more like wandering through the wilderness—much like the frontiersmen of the 1700s and 1800s did.

Rangers offer short guided hikes during the summer. Beginning at the Denali Park Hotel and the Eielson Visitor Center, these hikes range from thirty to ninety minutes. The rangers also lead longer "discovery hikes," which last for several hours. Hikers on these excursions must bring food, water, and hiking boots. They cross small streams and ascend rugged terrain.

If you want to hike, play, and sleep in Denali's backcountry, you must acquire a permit. To get a permit, you must watch the "backcountry simulator." This teaches you about backcountry safety, river crossings, and wildlife ethics. Denali's backcountry desk provides permits, maps, backcountry description guides, and a list of gear you should pack. Those who don't pack proper clothing, a compass, and other necessities are putting their lives in danger.

HUNTING FOR FISH

Alaska boasts some of the best fishing in the world. From its lakes, rivers, and the ocean, fishermen reel in giant salmon, trout, and halibut. Unfortunately, fishing in Denali is notoriously poor. The water is just too cold and contains too much glacial silt for fish to survive.

Some patient anglers catch arctic grayling in Denali's mountain streams or lake trout in Wonder Lake. But according to park rules, whatever they catch they have to throw back. A license is not required to fish in Denali.

BIKE AND HORSEBACK RIDING

At Denali, bicyclists have an advantage over drivers of automobiles: they can continue on the park road past Mile 14. However, no bike trails exist in Denali, and bicycles are not permitted in the backcountry.

With the rocky roads and steep terrain, biking isn't always fun—especially if a car sprays you with dirt and pebbles. Of course, nothing can beat the scenery.

Horseback riding is not permitted inside Denali. However, several companies allow tourists to explore the nearby area via horseback. Denali Saddle Safaris will take you on one-, two-, or four-hour tours, with the longer tours going higher into the mountains. Their four-hour expedition ($199) reaches 3,800 feet (1,158 meters). Boasts the company's Web site: "This tour covers it all—taiga, tundra, the alpine—from wildflowers to marmots, moose and bears. Snack provided (if you can eat it before your trusty horse does!)."[2]

⊜ WHITE-WATER RAFTING

Several companies offer white-water rafting opportunities on the Nenana River, which borders the park. Novices will want to choose the upper portion of the river, where the waters are tamer. Only the brave and the experienced should tackle the lower portion of the river. There, your raft plummets through the Nenana Canyon as you hang on for dear life. Children, wisely, are not allowed on the lower section of the river.

⊜ SLED DOG DEMOS

Here's an activity that is kid friendly. During the winter, rangers use dogsleds to patrol the park. In

A lonely pine tree stands out above Reflection Pond. There is not much good fishing to be done in Denali National Park. The water is simply too cold.

summer, they keep the dogs fit while entertaining the tourists with sled dog demonstrations. At a kennel near Mile 3, dogs are hooked up to a wheel-based sled. When the driver gives the command, the dogs bolt ahead at close to 20 miles per hour (32.2 kilometers per hour).

FLIGHTSEEING

This takes the Alaska experience to a higher level—figuratively and literally. From various airstrips and heliports, small aircraft will fly you above the Alaska Range. While those on earth are complaining that they can't get a good look at Mt. McKinley, you are circling around its pointy peaks. In fact, for $399 per person, Era Helicopters will transport you to high ground for a four-hour walk. Flightseeing is extremely expensive. But, advises Alaska.org, "[i]f you're going to make one splurge in Alaska, this should be it."[3]

CLIMBING MT. MCKINLEY

This "activity" is not for mere mortals. Only the most experienced and physically fit climbers should ever attempt to ascend the High One. Each year, more than a thousand adventurers make the attempt. The majority of them opt for the guided climb, which begins with an airlift to the 7,200-foot (2,195-meter) base camp on Kahiltna Glacier. From there, they try to ascend 13,000 more feet

(3,962 meters) to the summit. Though dressed as warmly as possible, most still get frostbite at the higher levels, where temperatures hover around –30°F (–34°C). About half the climbers achieve their goal, but in most years, at least one person dies in the attempt.

▲ *In the winter months, park rangers use dogsleds to patrol Denali.*

ENTERTAINMENT

Believe it or not, you can find a touch of Broadway in the Alaskan wilderness. The McKinley Chalet Resort hosts the Cabin Nite Dinner Theater. During their musical about the Kantishna gold rush, actors deliver plates of food right to your table. The Denali Princess Lodge offers its own dinner theater, staging *The Music of Denali*. This musical comedy recounts the first ascent of Mt. McKinley.

GOOD EATS

After forcing down a sack lunch during your bus trip through Denali, you'll want to enjoy a hearty meal as soon as you leave the park. Numerous restaurants offer a variety of delicious entrees, although your bill will be as big as your appetite. (Denali's entrance fees excluded, seemingly everything in Alaska is expensive.)

The Denali Salmon Bake in Glitter Gulch is a great place for salmon, king crab, and live music. Lynx Creek Pizza is *the* place—meaning the *only* place—to get pizza in the area. During the summer, this restaurant is packed day and night. For a fine-dining experience, check out The Summit Restaurant. You can enjoy steak and seafood while watching white-water rafters zip down the Nenana River. Many other restaurants can be found near Denali's entrance, in nearby Healy, and south of the park.

→OTHER ACTIVITIES AT DENALI

On May 15, 2007, the new Denali Visitor Center opened for its first full season. This 14,000-square foot (1,301-square meter) building is "eco-friendly." It was built with renewable wood products and heated in part by solar energy. Inside, tourists are wowed by a twenty-foot-high (6.1 meters), seventy-foot-long (21.3 meters) acrylic mural of Mt. McKinley painted on a curved wall. Equally cool are a twelve-foot-long (3.7-meter) model of the entire Denali NP&P and a fully dimensional wood puzzle called "What use is a moose?"

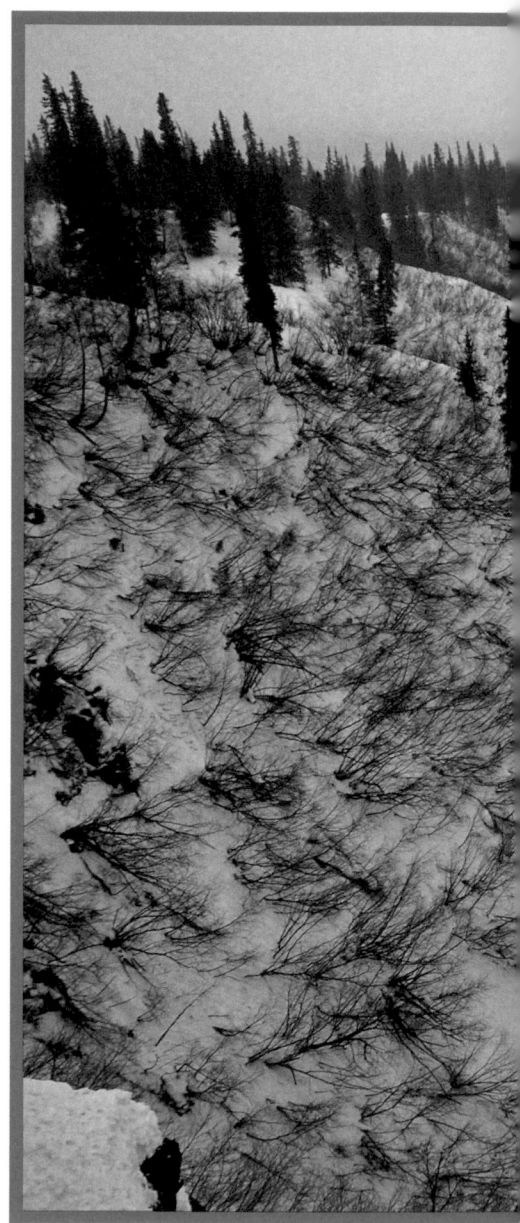

People explore Denali even in winter. Cross-country skiing and snowboarding have become increasingly popular. Visitors are allowed to ski on the park road, along sled dog trails, and in the back-country. No ski lifts exist in the park, and the upward climbs are tedious, but the descents are a heavenly reward.

Some visitors simply drive through Denali National Park and Preserve and then stop to look at the scenic vistas. This beautiful winter scene was shot from the side of the road.

The National Park Service developed the Junior Ranger Program to engage its young visitors. At Denali, kids can stop by the Visitor Center or the Talkeetna Ranger Station to get their free Junior Ranger Activity Guide. One guide is for kids ages nine to fourteen, and another is for tykes ages four to eight. The guides include activities and information about the park. Those who complete their activity guide need to show it to a park ranger. At that point, they are asked to recite the Junior Ranger Pledge and sign the Junior Ranger Certificate. Once they do, they receive their official Junior Ranger badge.

⊖ TAKE A DRIVE

Many places of note lie within two hundred miles of Denali NP&P's entrance. They include the town of North Pole, the Trans-Alaska Pipeline, the Big Delta State Historical Park, and the Wrangell-St. Elias National Park & Preserve. Many Denali visitors enjoy the northerly drive along the George Parks Highway to the city of Fairbanks. The views along the way are worth the trip to Alaska.

The highway straddles the Nenana River and climbs the Nenana River Canyon. The canyon walls contain mica, which makes the rock shine in the sunlight. En route to Fairbanks, you'll pass the Minto Flats State Game Refuge, the Purvis Lookout, and the Bonanza Creek Experimental Forest.

Mt. McKinley is visible on clear days, and sunsets paint the sky in shades of orange and yellow.

The 120-mile (193-kilometer) drive ends in Fairbanks, Alaska's second largest city with 31,000 residents. Highlights include the Georgeson Botanical Garden and its world-famous giant vegetables. Thanks to twenty hours of daylight in the summer, cabbages grow to the size of shrubbery. Bird watchers will want to check out Creamer's Field Migratory Waterfowl Refuge, an 1,800-acre (728-hectare) bird sanctuary.

DENALI STATE PARK

While Denali NP&P is bigger than Massachusetts, the Denali State Park is about half the size of Rhode Island. Established in 1970, the state park lies just east of its "big brother."

Denali State Park boasts terrain and wildlife similar to the national park, but it is different in several ways. First, it is a great place to fish. All five species of Pacific salmon live in the park's waters. So, too, do rainbow trout, arctic grayling, Dolly Varden, lake trout, burbot, and whitefish. Unlike at the national park, tourists can drive all the way through the Denali S.P., via the George Parks Highway. It is also a park less traveled. Tourists can enjoy the great outdoors and not have to contend with reservations, bus times, and other stresses associated with the national park.

TALKEETNA

This little town has been called South Denali Park because it is near the southern borders of both the national and state Denali parks. Fewer than five hundred people live in Talkeetna, but it is a quirky community that is worth a short visit. In fact, many believe the town was the inspiration for the popular television show *Northern Exposure.*

Talkeetna-based companies offer many ways to explore the region. These include flightseeing trips, Jeep tours, jet boat trips, fishing, and wagon rides. The town also hosts the annual Moose Dropping Festival and the Mountain Mother Contest. In the latter event, mothers test their wood-splitting ability and baby-diapering skills.

THE VACATION OF A LIFETIME

A trip to Denali National Park & Preserve represents "extreme travel." For most Americans, the park is extremely far away. The cost of the trip is exceptionally high, and in few places will you find so much daylight, such cold temperatures, and very high elevation. Yet the "extremes" make this trip the experience of a lifetime. So, too, do the pure and crisp air, towering mountain peaks, roar of the river, howl of the wolf, and explosion of colors.

On the Web site Epinions, twenty-eight of thirty-four visitors of Denali graded their vacation a "five" on a scale of one to five. Wrote one visitor:

Travel Alaska is the official Web site of the Alaska Travel Industry Association. Find out about activities at Denali and elsewhere in the state.

"Where else can you walk out your back door in the morning, be standing on a mountain and watching a grizzly bear eat his morning breakfast?"[4]

Only at Denali...

Report Links

The Internet sites described below can be accessed at
http://www.myreportlinks.com

▶**Denali National Park and Preserve**
Editor's Choice The official NPS Web site for Denali.

▶**Denali Biosphere Reserve Information**
Editor's Choice Find out why Denali was named a biosphere reserve.

▶**Denali Education Center**
Editor's Choice Make plans to explore Denali in person, or just learn about the plants and animal spec

▶**Denali: Alaska's Great Wilderness**
Editor's Choice A Web site about the changes that take place between seasons in Denali.

▶**Alaska State Division of Parks and Outdoor Recreation**
Editor's Choice Use this Web site to find other parks to visit in Alaska after a trip to Denali.

▶**Deadly Ascent**
Editor's Choice Learn how mountain climbing in Denali can affect the body.

▶**Alaska: Western Canada and United States Collection**
Bring Alaskan history to life with this collection of images, spanning 1745–1964.

▶**Alaska Maps**
See how the state of Alaska evolved and delve into detailed maps.

▶**Alaska's Digital Archives**
Alaska's rich culture and history are well documented by the state's digital archives.

▶**Alaska's History & Cultural Studies**
You can learn about each stage of Alaska's history through the materials presented on this site.

▶**Alaska Wildlife Alliance**
Read about an Alaskan group's efforts to preserve local plants, animals, and other wildlife.

▶**Athapascan Family**
This group populated the area near Denali from the last ice age until the 1900s.

▶**Brown Bear, Grizzly Bear**
Learn all about a common inhabitant of Denali, the grizzly bear.

▶**The Cretaceous**
Study the cretaceous period, the source of dinosaur remains found in Denali.

▶**Denali: Summit of North America, 6194m**
What does it take to climb to the top of Denali and the other members of the "7 Summits."

Report Links

The Internet sites described below can be accessed at
http://www.myreportlinks.com

▶**Denali Climbing History**
Learn about successful efforts to climb Mount McKinley.

▶**Eagles**
Two of the most popular birds in Alaska's skies are the bald eagle and the golden eagle.

▶**Illustrated Glossary of Alpine Glacial Landforms**
This educational Web site describes the variety of alpine glacial landforms.

▶**International Arctic Research Center**
Research efforts to address climate change in Alaska.

▶**Land Bridge to the New World**
Changes to the earth made it possible for humans to migrate by foot to North America.

▶**Meeting of the Frontiers**
Learn all about the meeting of the Russian-American frontier in Alaska.

▶*The Milepost*
Browse this site about travel in Alaska and the surrounding areas of Canada.

▶**Mount McKinley Weather Station**
Read about weather and efforts to measure it at an elevation of 19,000 feet (5,971 meters).

▶**National Parks Conservation Association**
This nonprofit group helps protect and preserve America's national parks.

▶**National Park Service**
Explore America's national parks with the official guide.

▶**Travel Alaska**
This state tourism site will help you explore Alaska's cities, towns, parks, and public lands.

▶**Tundra Ecoregions**
Denali is known for its tundra. Discover more about the tundra and other ecoregions.

▶**WebRangers**
Become a WebRanger by showing what you've learned about the national parks.

▶**Wildlife Notebook Series**
Get the facts on over one hundred species of animals and fish found at Denali.

▶**Wooly Mammoth**
Find out how the wooly mammoth made it to Alaska by browsing this Discovery Channel Web site.

alpine—Refers to a high mountain area where it is too cold for trees to grow.

angler—A person who uses a rod and reel to catch fish.

Arctic—The region within the Arctic Circle (includes the northern third of Alaska).

avalanche—A slide of snow and ice down a mountain.

chasm—A deep, steep-sided cleft in the earth's surface.

conservationist—A person who advocates the protection of natural resources.

ecology—The study of how organisms interact with each other and with their environment.

ecosystem—A community of organisms that interact with each other and the environment in which the organisms live.

environmentalist—A person who strives to protect the environment from pollution or destruction.

erosion—The wearing away of land or soil by wind, water, or glacial ice.

excavate—To dig something up.

expedition—A journey by a group of people that is organized for a particular purpose.

exotic plants—Plants that grow in a given place only as the result of human action.

fault—A fracture in the earth's crust.

glacier—An enormous mass of ice that moves slowly downslope due to its own weight.

granite—Hard rock consisting mostly of feldspar, quartz, and mica.

ice age—From thirty-five thousand to twelve thousand years ago, when enormous ice sheets covered much of North America.

industrialist—A person who plays a leading role in building up an industry.

mica—A group of minerals with a sheetlike crystal structure. Found in igneous and metamorphic rocks.

microorganism—An organism that can be seen only through a microscope.

migratory birds—Those that fly to a different location when the seasons change.

missionary—A person who tries to convert others to his or her religion.

naturalist—A person who studies and promotes nature.

paleontological—Pertaining to the study of fossils and extinct organisms.

plains—A vast area of flat land.

poacher—One who hunts or fishes illegally on another's property.

predator—An animal that seizes, kills, and eats other animals.

prospector—An explorer who looks for mineral deposits, such as gold.

sedimentary rock—Rock composed of sediment (solid particles and dissolved minerals).

seismic—Pertaining to earthquakes.

subarctic—The region just south of the Arctic Circle (includes the southern third of Alaska).

summit—The top of a mountain (n.). Ascending a mountain to its highest peak (v.).

taiga—A moist, subarctic forest of coniferous trees.

tectonic—Pertaining to movements in the earth's crust.

treeline—The point of elevation on mountains where tree growth ends.

tundra—A treeless plain in the arctic and subarctic regions.

vista—View.

wend—To travel on a course.

wilderness—Uninhabited land left in its natural condition.

wildflower—A flowering plant that grows on its own, without the help of people.

Chapter 1. The High One

1. Bill Sherwonit, *To the Top of Denali* (Seattle: Alaska Northwest Books, 1995), pp. 42–43.

2. Ibid., p. 52.

3. Ibid., p. 55.

4. Adam Randolph Collings, *Denali National Park, Mt. McKinley* (Anaheim, Calif.: Adam Randolph Collings, Inc., 1984), p. 49.

Chapter 2. Discovering Denali

1. Fred Beckey, *Mt. McKinley: Icy Crown of North America* (Seattle: The Mountaineers, 1998), p. 41.

2. Walter R. Borneman, *Alaska: Saga of a Bold Land* (New York: HarperCollins, 2003), p. 220.

3. Adam Randolph Collings, *Denali National Park, Mt. McKinley* (Anaheim, Calif.: Adam Randolph Collings, Inc., 1984), p. 20.

4. Ibid., p. 24.

5. Bill Sherwonit, *To the Top of Denali* (Seattle: Alaska Northwest Books, 1995), p. 57.

6. National Park Service, "Denali National Park Celebrates 90 Years!," *Denali National Park & Preserve,* n.d., <http://www.nps.gov/dena/denali-national-park-celebrates-90-years.htm> (July 2, 2007).

Chapter 3. Alaska's National Park

1. Kris Capps, *A Wildlife Guide: Denali National Park & Preserve, Alaska* (Santa Barbara, Calif.: ARA Leisure Services, 1994), pp. 6–8.

2. "People, Biodiversity, and Ecology," *UNESCO,* 1995–2007, <http://www.unesco.org/mab/ecosyst/urban/doc.shtml> (July 15, 2007).

Chapter 4. The Wild Life

1. National Park Service, "Lakes and Ponds," *Denali National Park & Preserve,* August 21, 2006, <http://www.nps.gov/dena/naturescience/lakesandponds.htm> (July 13, 2007).

2. "Just the Facts," *MountainZone.com,* n.d., <http://classic.mountainzone.com/climbing/99/denali/facts.html> (July 15, 2007).

3. BudinAk, "What do you consider 'cold'?" *City-Data.com,* May 14, 2007, <http://www.city-data.com/forum/alaska/81298-what-do-you-consider-cold-4.html> (July 17, 2007).

4. "Here are some Facts about Denali," *Climb for a Cure: Denali 2001,* April 23, 2004, <http://cancerclimb.thepeaks.com/facts.htm> (July 18, 2007).

5. National Park Service, "Black capped Chickadee," *Denali National Park & Preserve,* October 17, 2006, <http://www.nps.gov/dena/naturescience/chickadee.htm> (July 18, 2007).

Chapter 5. Big Issues

1. National Park Service, "Environmental Factors," Denali National Park & Preserve, August 21, 2006, <http://www.nps.gov/dena/naturescience/environmentalfactors.htm> (July 22, 2007).

2. Betsy51, "2 Mountaineers Die on Mt. McKinley," *topix.com,* May 19, 2007, <http://www.topix.net/forum/city/lake-forest-park-wa/TOEUMMP8N6PSBCTDD> (July 24, 2007).

3. climber, "2 Mountaineers Die on Mt. McKinley," *topix.com,* May 19, 2007, <http://www.topix.net/forum/city/lake-forest-park-wa/TOEUMMP8N6PSBCTDD> (July 24, 2007).

4. Jane Tranel, "'Dino-Mite' Discovery at Denali," *Alaska Region,* n.d., <http://www.nps.gov/akso/Press/2005/dinofinal.htm> (July 25, 2007).

5. Kate Golden, "Denali dino found," *Frontiersman,* July 8, 2005, <http://www.frontiersman.com/articles/2005/07/08/news/news2.txt> (August 14, 2008).

6. Adam Randolph Collings, *Denali National Park, Mt. McKinley* (Anaheim, Calif.: Adam Randolph Collings, Inc., 1984), p. 25.

Chapter 6. Exploring Denali

1. Heidi Leigh Johansen, ed. *Fodor's Alaska 2007* (New York: Random House, 2007), p. 382.

2. Dolly Varden Tours, "A Family Friendly Tour," *Denali: Horseback Riding,* 2008, <http://www.dollyvardenalaska.com/Denali%20Horseback%20Riding.htm> (August 14, 2008).

3. "Denali Flightseeing Tours," *Alaska.org,* n.d., <http://alaska.org/denali/flightseeing.htm> (August 3, 2007).

4. Batticia, "Do Denali," *Epinions.com,* November 16, 1999, <http://www1.epinions.com/trvl-review-62-F1D33CE-3831B25E-prod1> (August 4, 2007).

Beckman, Wendy Hart. *National Parks in Crisis: Debating the Issues.* Berkeley Heights, N.J.: Enslow Publishers, Inc., 2004.

Gill, Shelley. *Alaska.* Watertown, Mass.: Charlesbridge, 2007.

————, *Upon Denali: Alaska's Wild Mountain.* Seattle: Sasquatch Books, 2006.

Hall, M.C. *Welcome to Denali National Park.* Chanhassen, Minn.: Child's World, 2007.

Johansen, Heidi Leigh, ed. *Fodor's Alaska 2007.* New York: Random House, 2007.

Niz, Xavier W. *Alaska.* Mankato, Minn.: Capstone Press, 2003.

O'Donnell, Kerri. *Denali National Park, An Alaskan Ecosystem: Creating Graphical Representations of Data.* New York: PowerKids Press, 2007.

Staff. *Guide to the National Parks: Alaska.* Washington, D.C.: National Geographic Society, 2005.

Stefoff, Rebecca. *Alaska.* New York: Benchmark Books, 2000.

Stuck, Hudson. *Ascent of Denali.* Santa Barbara, Calif.: The Narrative Press, 2004.

Wohlforth, Charles. *Frommer's Alaska 2007.* Hoboken, N.J.: Wiley Publishing, Inc., 2007.